How To Make $100,000 Per Year Thanks To YouTube

LEARN HOW YOU CAN GET FREE TARGETED
TRAFFIC FROM VIDEOS

Gabriel Both

D1520856

Published by
Video Traffic Insider
Inspired Freedom LTD
Kemp House, 152 City Road
London, United Kingdom
EC1V 2NX

Book Layout ©2017 BookDesignTemplates.com

Disclaimer

Federal Trade Commission Disclosure

Disclosure of Material Connection: Some of the links contained in this book are "affiliate links." This means if you visit the link and purchase the item, then the author will receive an affiliate commission. We are disclosing this in accordance with the Federal Trade Commission's 16 CFR, Part 255: "Guides Concerning the Use of Endorsements and Testimonials in Advertising.

Contents

Deep gratitude goes to:

My 'Laptop Millionaire Mentor' Mark Anastasi, Pegah who helped me to get into the program, my loving and supportive parents, and all of my close friends who believed in me all along my journey.

CHAPTER 1

Introduction

There may be many reasons why you chose to pick up and read this book. Maybe it was the title that grabbed you and you want to learn how to make $100,000+ per year thanks to YouTube, like many of the experts I have interviewed have done.

Maybe you're looking simply to get more free, targeted traffic to your websites thanks to videos. That's perfect, I've packed it full of strategies and tactics that you can implement right away and start getting measureable results.

Maybe you're reading this because you're interested in the stories of the experts that I've interviewed over the months, who will share with you how they got to where they are now in their business thanks to YouTube.

Or maybe, someone gave you this book or recommended it to you and you just want to learn how you can make more money online.

Who This Book Is For

This book is for anyone who is serious about making money and building a business through YouTube. Whether you are still employed full time, or already a solopreneur or small business owner, this book will help you get the results you seek.

It's also for anybody who has tried YouTube before, but hasn't had much success with it and has lost hope or even given up entirely.

It assumes that you have basic knowledge of how to use a computer, how to operate a camera or smartphone and have an open mind with an attitude of learning.

This book doesn't assume any existing technical knowledge, but if you already do have it, that will accelerate your progress. You will need a computer from within the last 1-2 years maximum which should be powerful enough to edit and process videos, and a decent internet connection which can upload files at a reasonable speed.

Even if you do have "knowledge gaps", you'll be able to still achieve the aims because I will guide you through the process and explain the different technical terms and concepts.

What You Will Get from This Book

My big promise to you is that if you apply the information in this book consistently, you **will** get results - whether that is in the form of more free traffic, more leads, more sales, or even creating a 6-figure business using YouTube.

Multiple experts have been interviewed throughout this book, and each will have a dedicated chapter to let you in on their top YouTube secrets, specific strategies, and tactics that you can apply right away.

You'll also be able to get into the mindset of these successful YouTubers to model their methods.

Additionally, I have added a lot of great tools, resources, and links to extra digital media that you can access on the website. For example, most of the experts will have a link to the video interview you can watch online.

Most of the links have been shortened from videotrafficinsider.com to vidtr.in, which makes it easier for you to type into your browser.

Why I Wrote This Book

I wrote this book with the purpose to both inspire and educate; to open your eyes and show you what is really possible in life thanks to having an online business. I remember many books that have changed my life, because they shifted my mindset, shattered my old limiting beliefs, and showed me another way that was way better than I had ever imagined.

I've already seen incredible results in just 3 months of starting my channels, and those results will continue to expand and accelerate with time and consistent effort.

At the time of the launch of this book, I will have officially resigned from my 9-5 job and be a full-time YouTube expert & entrepreneur.

That's how confident I am in the information I'm about to share with you here. I'm not suggesting you do the same, but for my own situation, I felt this to be the best decision and perfect timing.

The best outcome I would want for you is that after reading this, you have a renewed sense of hope that you too can live life on your own terms and that you now have the tools, strategies, and resources to start walking on that path and getting the results you want.

Maybe you're in a 9-5 day job, feeling unhappy, unfulfilled, underappreciated, underpaid, stuck and trapped in the rat race... or maybe you're already an entrepreneur who just wants to find a more effective and efficient way grow your business.

Whatever your background, it doesn't matter. The fact is you're most likely struggling in some way and are looking for answers and solutions. I'll do my best to serve you and help you find what you're looking for throughout these pages.

I want to congratulate you. Don't take the fact that you're reading this book for granted. You're far ahead of most people who just "wish" their life to be better, but who never take action to move ahead.

Everybody wants to make more money, look sexy, and find the love of their life, but very few will do much about it, and even fewer will persist and never give up until they get exactly what they want.

Let me tell you something - writing this book did not come easy, but I made it happen. Where most people would find an excuse, I found a way. Remember this for yourself when you start on your journey.

How I Wrote This Book

I wrote this book while I was working full time as an SEO Account Manager in London, 8.5 hours plus 3 hours of commuting every single day, 5 days a week. I left my flat at 7:30am in the morning and came home around 7:30pm at night, exhausted.

That left me with only a few hours after dinner and daily tasks to focus on building my business, and writing this book. There wasn't enough time during the week, so I had to be more creative…

While I was writing this book, I wasn't yet earning enough money from YouTube to justify resigning my job, so I had to stick it out for a bit longer until I felt the income was enough to cover my basic needs.

I crammed the interviews for the experts into the evenings and weekends, then did the audio transcribing on my laptop as I was on the bus and train to and from work. I wrote most of the book during this time. That gave me about 2 hours extra productivity per day.

Then, I also made full use of my 1-hour lunch breaks and went to a café to work there.

I remember having to even do a few interviews in the café as well because it was the only time that worked some days. One time, the Wi-Fi there stopped working, so I managed last minute to connect to the Internet using my mobile network connection so I could do a live YouTube video interview in time. Man, that was nuts!

I worked most of the weekend as well, so pretty much every spare hour was being used up to work on this book and work on my business.

The reason I shared this story with you was for two reasons:

Firstly, so you can see how much love, commitment, and care I put into creating this book for you and that I truly want to make a positive difference in your life and your business.

Secondly, so you realize that you too can succeed, no matter what your current situation is. Every obstacle can be overcome!

How To Read This Book

I have divided the book into 4 core parts:

Part one is the foundation and introduces you to my story, learning the basic business concepts, and then introduces you to some of the top YouTube myths a lot of people have.

Part two is the nitty gritty YouTube strategies. This is specific information you can start applying right away and get noticeable improvements in your video views, engagement, and traffic.

Part three revolves around the experts I've interviewed. The interviews have been transcribed and rewritten so that they are easier to read and I've also highlighted important pieces of information they share.

From time to time, I will expand and digress on certain key points and topics that the experts talk about so you understand it better and can follow the specific techniques.

Most of the interviews have a link to an exclusive YouTube VIP video interview recording, which you can watch or listen to as an extra.

Part four is about mastering your mindset and taking the next steps to make even faster progress. If you're not confident in your abilities to achieve the results you want or if you find you get stuck, then I would recommend reading the mindset chapter first. This is the real key to lasting success. I'll also share with you my experience of a 30-day challenge and give you an opportunity to start with your own.

For any technical terms that you do not understand, I have included a **glossary** at the end of the book that you can refer to.

To get the most out of this book, I recommend reading it from front to back, but if you prefer to jump to a specific section and read from there, that works just as well.

Throughout this book, you'll see different symbols for different pieces of information. Here is a quick overview of them:

 This will point out a tip, which will highlight a piece of info.

 A super tip is intended to be more powerful than a normal tip.

 This is an important symbol, which makes you aware of some important piece of information you should remember.

 An action step is information you can apply right away.

 Tools & resources are links to software tools, equipment, or additional resources you can use to help with your journey.

 This refers to a list of ideas that you can use or get inspiration from.

 The additional content icon refers to extra material you can access online or on the website.

With that being said, enjoy, and I hope you find lots of value in it so you can get the results you are looking for.

To Your Success,

Gabriel Both

Follow Me Here:

Add me on Facebook: @gabe.both
Follow me on Twitter: @Gabe_Both
Follow me on Instagram: @gabrielboth

My YouTube Channels:

Video Traffic Insider: vidtr.in/vti
Internet Marketing Tutorials: vidtr.in/imt
Maximum You: vidtr.in/my

CHAPTER 2

Why YouTube?

Why from all the other ways I could make money online did I choose YouTube? That's a great question, because the fact is, there are thousands of ways to make money online.

More and more people are waking up every day to the unlimited opportunities that are on the Internet.

Becoming an entrepreneur is an increasing trend that's pretty trendy right now. Businesses that are not on YouTube are ignoring a huge untapped opportunity to generate free traffic, leads, and sales.

I've always found it hard to commit to one specific craft and I felt that I would confine myself too much. This is a common problem with a lot of creative people, but my mentor Mark Anastasi said you've got to specialize in ONE thing, become really good at it, and master it. Then you can always move on to something else later.

I've always loved working with video as a media format and produced many videos in my spare time. I've tried blogging for many years, but I've always felt writing was difficult and tedious - in short, I didn't enjoy it.

When Mark gave me the task of a 30-Day YouTube Challenge, at first I didn't want to take it on. It seemed "impossible" to create 360 YouTube videos with 30 niche blogs and 150 articles all in 30 days.

In fact, the first few days, I nearly gave up...

BUT, then after a few days of vacillating between decisions, I decided to take on the challenge and I actually really enjoyed creating videos, sharing knowledge, and seeing that it helped people. That's what fired me up, and I decided then that YouTube would be my niche that I focus on. I'm now extremely passionate about it.

By now you're probably wondering "OK, so what about me? Why should I do YouTube?"

Thanks for asking, I'm going to show you why now is one of the best times to make money on YouTube and fill you in on all the market statistics to show you why it's THE way to go versus all the other opportunities out there.

The Second Largest Search Engine in the World

YouTube is, believe it or not, the second largest search engine in the world, second to Google. It's also the third most visited site after Google and Facebook.

On February 14th, 2005 (yes, Valentine's Day), the domain "YouTube.com" was activated and the company got started.

Only nine weeks later on April 23rd, the first ever YouTube video was uploaded by co-founder Jawed Karim, called "Me at the Zoo" at the San Diego Zoo in California.

On October 9, 2006 that it was announced that YouTube would be purchased by Google for a whopping $1.65 billion USD.

That's less than 2 years after it started.

The first paid adverts were rolled out in August 2007, opening up another opportunity for Internet marketers to take advantage of and reach a larger audience on demand.

YouTube Quick Facts*

According to Brandwatch.com, here are some of the reasons why you've got to hop on the YouTube train NOW rather than later:

- Every 6 out of 10 people **prefer online video platforms** to live TV.
- It's predicted that **half of viewers under 32** will **not** use a paid TV service by 2025.
- **80% of 18-49 year-olds watch YouTube videos** in an average month and on mobile alone, YouTube reaches more of this age group than any broadcast or cable TV network.
- In 2015, **watch time increased 74%** on YouTube and 18-49 year-olds spent 4% less time watching TV.
- YouTube has support for **over 76 different languages**, which covers 95% of the Internet users, making it accessible worldwide.
- As of the publication of this book, PewDiePie (Felix Kjellberg) is the highest earning YouTube star with over **43 million subscribers, earning $12 million** (before tax) in 2015.

Can you start seeing the huge potential of this global social media platform? Check out some of the usage statistics:

- Every minute, over **300 minutes of video** are uploaded to YouTube.
- Every day, there are over **1,000,000,000 mobile video views.**
- Every month, **3.25 billion hours** of video are watched.
- Over half of YouTube views come from mobile devices and this trend is increasing.
- The average viewing session on mobile devices on YouTube is **40 minutes**.
- Animated explainer videos **increase conversion rates by 20%** according to Unbounce.

Here are some more shocking YouTube marketing statistics:

- YouTube accounts for **two thirds of the premium online video watched across devices,** among millennials.
- Only **9% of U.S. small businesses** use YouTube.
- The number of YouTube **channels earning six figures each year** on YouTube has increased by 50% year on year.
- In 2014, **4 of the top 10 videos were adverts**.
- The most viewed brand videos are an average of **31-60 seconds long (32% of all views)**.
- The same brands have an average of **2.4 channels**.
- Searches of **"how to" videos on YouTube are growing 70%** year on year.
- **96% of B2B organizations** use video in some capacity in their marketing campaigns of which **73% report positive results to their ROI**, according to a survey conducted by ReelSEO.
- According to an Australian Retailer, real estate listings that include a video **receive 403% more inquiries** than those without.

YouTube TrueView Ads facts:

- Viewers who watched at least 30 seconds or to completion of TrueView ads, were **23 times more likely to visit or subscribe to a brand channel, watch more by that brand, or share the brand video.**
- The viewers who were exposed to TrueView ads but didn't watch until completion, are **still 10 times more likely to take one of those actions.**
- When brands use TrueView, they see **views of previously existing content increase by up to 500%** after posting new videos.

*Facts Source: vidtr.in/bws

I hope now you can see the potential and amazing opportunity that YouTube offers, now and in the future. If I were you, I'd take advantage of it, and leverage the platform to grow your business and brand, and create and share the life of your dreams.

PART 1:
THE FOUNDATION

CHAPTER 3

Understanding the Basics

I f you're new to internet marketing or business in general, I figured it would be a good idea to go over some basic concepts that will help you to understand the big picture of internet marketing.

Most people coming into this industry approach Internet marketing completely the wrong way and don't have the right idea of what some of these core business concepts really are. This lack of knowledge will only lead to more failures and frustration.

I remember before I first started, I thought marketing was all about adverts and selling, which in my mind really meant pitching and "pushing" someone to buy something they may or may not really need. A lot of people have that idea, but it's the wrong mindset completely. Let me explain...

Let's start out by talking about the "lifeblood" of all businesses and the economy – money. This word can evoke negative emotions in a lot of people, but it's rather a lack of understanding and our upbringing that created this mindset.

Money is simply energy and the measure of the value that you create, which is determined by what the market currently views as valuable. It's simply just a physical and measurable way to show how much we or someone else values something.

Important: *Money is neither good nor bad, it just magnifies more of who we already are.*

What Is Value?

This can be subjective, but usually it's a solution to a problem, answer to a question, or something that brings a benefit to someone or something. In other words anything that leaves someone or something in a better place than before.

Believe it or not, how much money you have in your bank account right now is more or less how much value (or perceived value) you've delivered to society. The question you really need to ask yourself is how many people are you serving and how much value are you serving them?

For example, let's take movie stars. They get paid millions of dollars a year. Why? Because they are delivering value to millions of people through their movies.

Then you may ask what about, for example, nursing and emergency services staff, who also deliver a lot of value by saving people's lives. Why don't they get paid millions?

The limiting factor is the system they are working within, which pays them a salary instead of the results they deliver. They are also limited by the number of people they can serve at a time because they need to be there in person and there are only so many hours in a day.

Here's another way of looking at it...

Let's say you're currently working at a 9-5 day job. You're delivering value to your employer, your co-workers, and maybe a handful of clients. So it's no surprise that the salary you're earning is capped at where it is. You are only serving a limited number of people. Therefore, the company is only earning a certain amount and can only afford to pay you a certain salary.

The problem is, you have very little control over what you can earn at that company because you're in a very small "marketplace" and most likely have limited influence over the direction, policies, and other areas of the company.

The only way to have uncapped and unlimited potential for delivering more value is through having your own business(es). This is where you have the most control over your future and your finances.

What is a business? A business is simply a "vehicle" that delivers something of value to a customer (either a consumer or other business).

To recap quickly: You have something of value that people or businesses would exchange money for, and you have a business that delivers that value to that audience. The only thing is how do you let that audience know that you have something of value to deliver to them?

What Is Marketing?

Marketing delivers the message between a business and an audience. The purpose is to make the audience aware that "Hey, you have something of value that the audience wants or needs!".

There are so many "channels" or ways to reach audiences, and thanks to the Internet, the costs and risks of doing so can be virtually none.

This provides an incredible opportunity for anyone with an Internet connection and something of value to share, to create a thriving business, anywhere in the world.

What Is Sales?

The final step of the process is sales. Once the audience is aware that there is something of value that can help them in some form, the only way for that exchange to happen is through a sale. If you just remember one thing about sales is that SELLING = SERVING.

The process of sales is simply the way that you show someone the benefits of the product or service so they see that the money they exchange for it is a fair trade.

 Important: *If you give something away for free that has value, it's not a business - it's a charity. And although charities are great, by giving away something of value for free, there is an imbalance of energy created. What also can happen is as a result, people don't value it as much or don't take it seriously.*

That's why Sales is so important! It makes it possible for a balanced and sustainable exchange of energy and it's critical for any business that wants to keep alive in the long term.

I want to introduce one final important concept that you'll definitely need to know if you want to be able to deliver even more value to more people and make a lot of money.

What Is Leverage?

Think of a lever – a tool where through small input, one can achieve a greater output.

For example, let's say your outcome is to share the solutions to "losing weight naturally" to 1,000 people. You could do 1-on-1 coaching to deliver that value, but it would take a long time to reach 1,000 people, right? Even if you charged $1,000 for a 1-hour session, the time it takes still stays the same. Doing it this way, you would be using very little leverage.

Now, imagine if you recorded yourself on video and covered all the solutions and answers to questions that your clients would ask. You create a "home study course" and put the videos on a membership site online where your clients can access 24/7, whenever they want.

You can now serve 1,000 clients simultaneously, without requiring any of your time. You're now using massive leverage, thanks to technology and the Internet.

Do you see how powerful it is now to use leverage in your business?

It can mean the difference between creating a job for yourself or you having the freedom to work only a few hours a week, only when you want to.

CHAPTER 4

My Story

I added this chapter so you could get a glimpse into my life and get to know me a bit more. I share my story to inspire you and give you hope that you too can overcome the darkest of struggles and create the life you really want and deserve.

In this chapter, you may read about terms or concepts you're not yet familiar with yet, but rest assured that however overwhelming it may seem now, these are things that you'll be able to learn later in the book when I reveal them in more detail.

How I Found My Laptop Millionaire Mentor

I grew up in a small town called Wolfville in Nova Scotia, Canada. It is a university town, home of Acadia University. My dad was a Professor of Music there and so it was quite natural for me to study there after I graduated from high school.

I got into computers at a very early age, right about the time when Windows 95 came out and dial-up was the only way to get online at home.

Over the years, I become a self-learned expert at computers, I built my own machines and was deep into high performance PC gaming.

After high school I signed up to do my Bachelors of Computer Science degree at Acadia University in 2009. I must admit, not only did I learn a lot during those 5 years, but I went through a complete personal transformation – from being one of the biggest partiers in my residence to discovering the world of personal development, to quitting alcohol for life, discovering the possibilities of internet marketing and online business and starting my own digital media agency.

I could write several books about my journey during those years, but for the sake of keeping it short, I'll mention the most significant turning points.

My first major turning point was halfway through my first year of university. I stumbled across this book called "Study Smarter Not Harder" by Jaico Publishing House, and I had this paradigm breakthrough where I realized I could improve my performance way beyond what I ever thought or what the general population believed was possible. It was a real eye opener!

*That book started my thirst for learning more about accelerated learning. After lots of research online, I came across this incredible personal development blog called **Personal Development For Smart People** by Steve Pavlina (stevepavlina.com). Check it out - it rocks.*

This blog really opened me up to the world of personal development and inspired me to do even more reading in this field.

Soon, I was reading books by Wayne Dyer, Joe Dispenza, Paul Scheele, Anthony Robbins, and countless others.

I joined a local newly formed Toastmasters (toastmasters.org) club, which is an international non-profit organization to help people improve their public speaking and leadership skills. I was the first in the club to do my first 10 public speeches.

I later went on to become the president of the club and with the help of the members and more experienced Toastmasters, managed to charter the club as an official Toastmasters International club.

I was able to go from being a super shy and socially anxious teen who was terrified of speaking in public, to a confident young man who enjoyed speaking in front of an audience. This club helped me to grow a lot in so many ways.

My second major turning point was during my second year of university when I had a really intense and scary experience...

I had a massive anxiety attack due to a substance, and for a week afterwards I was in a state of derealization or depersonalization where I felt I was seeing my reality through a glass pane. It was super frightening, but fortunately, I was mostly able to snap out of it a week later. It took me over a year to feel normal again.

I made a vow to myself never to touch ANY drugs ever again, including alcohol. So I went cold turkey and quit completely. I've been 100% clean since 2013.

My third major turning point was during my third year of university when a few significant events happened.

That year I found my spiritual path and I started to meditate daily.

My dad's friend introduced me to an online Internet marketing community called "The Daily Marketing Coach" or DMC lead by 8-figure earner Ann Sieg. That's where I started my Internet marketing journey.

That same year in 2013, I created my own local personal development club that grew into a small, 4-person group and in that group, one of the members recommended a book called **The Laptop Millionaire** by Mark

Anastasi. Little did I know, but **this book would change the direction of my life.**

I read the book and it shattered my old conditioning I had about what is possible in life and in my career. It opened my eyes to the fact that I don't have to be in a time-consuming job that I hate, for the rest of my life – instead I could do what I love and make 10x, 100x, or even 1,000x more money, in way less time and actually LIVE life and enjoy it, thanks to the power of the internet.

From that point onwards this became my goal – to master the art of internet marketing and become financially free so I could have the time, resources, and leverage to make a massive positive difference in millions of people's lives all around the world.

I made up my mind that I wanted Mark to be my #1 Internet marketing mentor and wanted to be personally coached by him. I had no idea at that time that literally just 2 years later, I would move to London, UK, meet Mark himself at a live seminar, and then get selected as one of 12 people out of hundreds of others to get mentored by him one on one.

You know what's crazy, that's exactly what happened! You're probably thinking, "Wow, great for you, you're lucky...". Let me tell you, luck has nothing to do with it. In fact, between the time when I was given his book and now, as I am writing this one with the guidance of Mark, I experienced a lot of challenges, hardships, and failures that forced me to learn, grow, and change into the person I needed to become to be able to do what I do now.

30

For example, the primary reason why I moved to London was because I got into a long distance relationship and moved to London to live with her. We got engaged, but I soon realized that we were not compatible for the long term and 2 ½ years later, I decided the best thing for both of us would be to say farewell and move on.

During those years, I found myself "job jumping" every 3-6 months because I hated working at a job so much. I needed to pay the bills, but at the same time, I hadn't yet been able to get my business off the ground for some reason. Something was stopping me. Deep inside I knew I had limiting beliefs about money, wealth, success that were subconsciously stopping me from moving forward. I had to find a way...

I got deeper and deeper into debt and maxed out every credit card I had. I was around £30,000 in debt, paying about £900 a month in loan repayments and interest, which was almost half my salary.

I literally had no money left to dig myself out of this mess. I was completely trapped financially and realized it would take DECADES to dig myself out of this at that rate. I knew I MUST find a way to create a successful business to become free as soon as possible.

During those years, my health was suffering and I was going downhill in many areas of my life. I had severe chronic fatigue and struggled with my energy levels, which was a real challenge because I needed to work on my own business projects I was doing at the time, to move ahead.

The Facebook Post That Changed My Life

Shortly after my ex-fiancé and I broke up in July 2016, I saw a Facebook post from Mark Anastasi, who offered to help 12 people to get to $100k in 12 months, guaranteed! or money back.

This was the opportunity I was waiting for, and it was such an unbelievably incredible offer, there was no way I was going to miss out on it.

The only challenge was, I was still deep in debt and somehow needed to raise £4,700 to qualify for the program. I didn't know how I was going to do it, but I grabbed the opportunity, trusting that it would work out if it was meant to be. Normally, he would charge clients £20,000+ for a year of 1-on-1 mentoring.

I contacted Mark and emailed him a long message letting him know why I should be one of the 12 selected candidates. I poured my heart into it and did everything I could to show him I will make the most of this and reach the goal if I'm selected.

A few days later, I got a message back from him asking when I was free for an interview. We scheduled a day and time for July 6th, 2016. I was thrilled!

The interview lasted about 40 minutes and was mostly for him to see the reason(s) why I wanted to reach $100k+ and see whether it aligned with what he was looking for in the candidates.

I think he really liked my answers because the call went on longer than expected and he gave me lots of tips and ways how I could generate the money I needed to join the program by July 26th. I remember he said, "Your greatest resource is your resourcefulness". I had to find a way no matter what...

I brainstormed a long list of different ways I could make the money, but was slightly hesitant to start taking action because the final selection hadn't been made yet.

I asked him when I would hear about the final decision and he said it would be in about a week. He had received hundreds of messages and out of those, only selected about 60 to interview to choose 12 from.

I remember clearly that on the morning of July 19th, 2016, when the decision was to be announced, I did something really powerful. I decided to visualize myself already having been selected as one of the 12 candidates. I said thank you to the universe in advance for giving me this opportunity. I really tapped into feeling the emotion of having being selected. I imagined myself working with Mark and becoming financially free, travelling the world. I was being grateful for something that had not yet manifested, but that I was 100% certain would become reality.

That day, I never received an email in my inbox.

I was beginning to think that I had not been chosen, but I decided to wait a few more days just in case he was delayed in the process.

I believe it was Thursday, two days later, that I checked my spam folder and low and behold, there was the email:

"Congratulations! You have been selected to be among the 12 people that will join me for my new "$100,000 in 12 Months" Laptop Millionaire program!"

I was absolutely blown away! Wow, I'm in! I now only had 5 days to come up with money so I could get started.

I Learn to Become More Resourceful

I went back to the list and took massive action. I applied to some bank loans but they all turned me down. I called up some of my close friends and asked them if they could lend me the money.

I posted on my Facebook page to see whether anyone knew any investors. One of my friends text me saying he had a friend who was an investor and gave me his contact details.

I wrote up a 6-page business plan from a template Mark had given me, in a few hours and sent it to him.

A few days went by and time was running out. The investor turned down my offer, so I realized that maybe instead of asking for money, I need to first GIVE massive value.

I decided to create a super irresistible website and SEO package offer worth over $2,000 and price it for only $150. I would post it on my Facebook and a few active groups I was in. I received a flood of enquiries and within less than 48 hours, I had made over £500.

I was still short 90% of the money. I was getting desperate and started to research high interest guarantor loans and even (dare I say!) pay-day loans, which I knew I should never ever touch, but something inside me said this opportunity is gold and I MUST make it happen, whatever the cost.

I called up some more people I knew but none of them agreed to be a guarantor for the loan. I was out of options.

There was only 1 day left, and I remember clearly, I was riding back from work on the bus and this wave of anger and frustration hit me like a wall. It was really intense and I couldn't help but cry.

"Why wasn't anything working?", "I deserve this opportunity, will I even find the money for this?!", "It's not fair!", "All these people with money and they don't lend it to someone who will do so much good with it!" and thoughts like these. I felt defeated...

I was texting with my ex-fiancé as we were still in touch and she asked me how I was doing. I told her.

She called and was wondering what the matter was. I didn't want to tell her, but she managed to open me up and I told her I needed to find the money by tomorrow so I could reach $100k in 12 months with Mark Anastasi.

Her response came completely unexpected. She said, "No problem, I can help you, I'll be your guarantor."

I was so grateful and hope flooded back in. I emailed Mark asking whether I could get an extension on the deadline for the funds. He kindly gave me until the end of the month.

It's interesting... the people I thought who would most likely help me, didn't and the ones I least expected to help me, did or at least supported me in some way or another. It was during these times I realized that I know my true friends.

The next morning I did my morning meditation as I usually do, and I let myself be open to be guided to an answer.

Suddenly a clear image and thought appeared and crystallized in my mind. It blew me away at the profound message I received.

In order for me to reach the goal, I must be willing to accept where I'm at right now (the present moment, [the dot]), and then accept and surrender to both possible outcomes that it may work out, or may not work out (future possibilities, [right and left arrows]).

Only then, can there be true calm inside me and the gate can be unlocked to the path that leads to the best possible outcome.

That day I truly felt like everything was going to work out for the best, whatever the result was.

I applied to a few guarantor loans and all but one turned me down. I was hanging on by a thread of hope that this one remaining bank would approve the loan.

It was on the day of the extended deadline: July 29th, 2016 that the loan was approved and I was able to secure the funds and send it over to Mark. I had made it and was officially in the $100k program!

Money Mindset Transformation

The first month of the program was all about transforming my mindset (see relevant chapter for how to do this yourself). It was about getting rid of all the internal blocks and limiting beliefs that had stopped me all along from becoming successful, despite all my hard work and efforts.

My mind was running on "old software" and I needed to upgrade my neural wiring so I could start attracting the abundance and wealth that was there all along.

I dove deep into the dark areas of my mind and discovered a ton of limiting beliefs about money, success, wealth, and abundance.

I also did two very powerful exercises, which were to write down **100 Reasons WHY I Must Make £20,000 a Month** (this was my number). The other exercise was to write down **100 Ways HOW I Can Make £20,000 a Month**. I highly recommend you do the same exercises to radically transform your mindset.

Both exercises were very challenging and forced my brain to keep tapping deeper into my creativity and come up with ideas. It took me several days to complete both lists, but the fact was I finished them.

There were several points where I drew blanks, but I kept pushing onwards until I reached the end.

I listened daily to an abundance subliminal track and did affirmations and other mindset exercises to condition my subconscious mind.

I knew that if I kept going like this, eventually, I would have completely rewired my brain with a new mindset that will get me the results I want.

During the second month, we were tasked with coming up with our business niche and Million Dollar Marketing Hook. This was to be our "backbone" of our business and would serve to define our target audience, the big problem we would solve for them, and to grab their attention to get them into our marketing funnel.

I struggled long and hard trying to choose a niche I wanted to commit to. The problem was, I have so many interests and passions that I didn't want to give up everything else. This made it very hard to choose.

Weeks later, I still couldn't make up my mind on which niche I wanted to focus on - Blogging? Twitter? Facebook? Email marketing? YouTube? I didn't want to leave anything out.

I realized this belief was exactly what was holding me back all these years from becoming successful - I was doing too many things at once because of the fear of missing out, and ended up becoming a master of none!

Everyone else on the program decided to interview experts for their main product. I wanted to do the same - it sounded fun and easy, but Mark suggested that I do a 30-day challenge with the goal of generating $1,000 in 30 days thanks to traffic from YouTube.

I subconsciously avoided his idea and kept suggesting niches and marketing hooks that "sounded cool" but didn't have a big problem to solve, or were not going to make me money.

Eventually, Mark's persistence paid off, and I finally said, "OK, I'll do the 30-day challenge, you're my mentor, you know best, I'll do it."

If you want to learn more about my experience of the 30-day challenge or want some guidance on how to start with your own, I invite you to read that chapter in part 4.

The next challenge was to work towards getting a total of 400 clicks per day from YouTube videos or other online sources and learn how to rank YouTube videos, both on YouTube itself and on Google.

I Master Ranking on YouTube

I decided the best and fastest way forward would be to model someone else who has already achieved what I'm looking to do, so I started looking for YouTube video ranking courses.

I decided to first search YouTube itself and soon stumbled across Michael Koehler's video (see Michael Koehler's chapter). I bought his course, studied it within a few days, and started applying it right away.

I decided to create a new YouTube channel that was a fresh start from the 360 crappy videos I had created the month before. I wanted to be able to promote Internet marketing products and tools that I have used myself in the past, so I decided to create the channel "Internet Marketing Tutorials" (@InternetMarketingTutorials).

I created about 1 video per day in the beginning and started tracking the video keyword positions in the rank tracking software I was using.

A few days later, I checked my stats and I couldn't believe it, I was ranking on the first page for some pretty good keywords!

The rankings increased steadily over the months, here a few examples of my ranking positions over time:

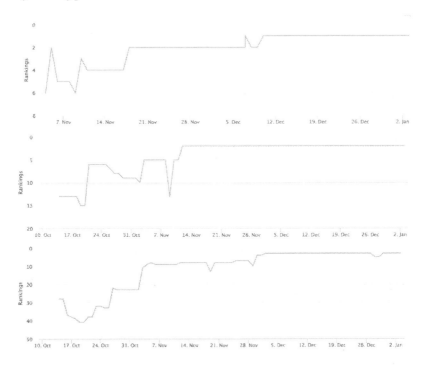

I was able to rank for over 25% of all my keywords in the first 1-3 positions and over 50% in the first 10 positions.

The amount of views and free traffic I was getting was amazing; I had never in my life gotten these kinds of numbers. Here are some more insider stats from my channel.

Within 57 days, I hit 100 subscribers, and in less than 3 months I reached over 180, which is almost double. That may not seem a lot, but keep in mind,

I hardly added any videos for over a month, and that's with only 32 total videos. Pretty decent!

Here were some of my top performing videos:

I was getting around 250 views a day on my channel:

Last 48 hours

Estimated views: 500

Again, maybe not a lot to start with, but that's with no maintenance and no regular posting, all organic views.

Let's take a look at the clicks:

For one of my videos, I was getting about 200 clicks a month, or between 6 and 7 clicks per day.

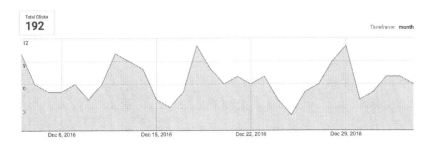

On another video, I was getting about 130 clicks a months, or about 4 per day. Not a whole lot, but still, it added up over time.

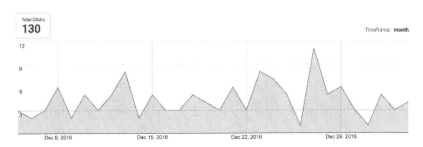

Comments were flooding into my inbox, and I was getting lots of interaction on my videos.

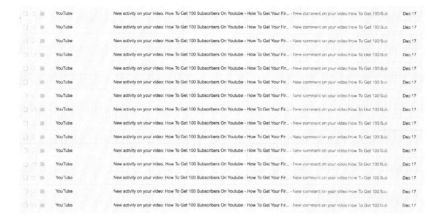

And yes, the day finally came when I made money on YouTube...

I Make My First Affiliate Sales on YouTube

One day, I logged into my affiliate dashboards (this is where you log into your affiliate account to see your stats and commissions) and low and behold, I had made a few sales (2 x $11) on one of the products I promoting!

This was thanks to my video "How To Get Twitter Followers Fast" that was getting around 50 views a day.

Soon, I was making affiliate sales on other products as well:

Date	Service	Paid	Your commission	Status
2016-12-22 16:29:45 UTC	KWFinder Premium	$45.00	$13.50	PENDING
2016-12-21 00:26:11 UTC	KWFinder Basic	$29.00	$8.70	PENDING

Date	Status	Sub-Affiliate ID	Commission	View Details
11-27-2016	Approved - Pending Payment	N/A	$33.50 USD	View Details
11-21-2016	Approved - Pending Payment	N/A	$33.50 USD	View Details

Showing 1 to 10 of 18 entries

Signup Date	Product/Service	Amount	Commission	Status
12/17/2016	SSD1G	$7.00 USD Monthly	$1.05 USD	Active
12/08/2016	SSD1G	$9.00 USD Monthly	$1.35 USD	Active
12/08/2016	SSD1G	$7.00 USD Monthly	$1.05 USD	Active
12/08/2016	SSD1G	$9.00 USD Monthly	$1.35 USD	Active
12/08/2016	SSD4G	$15.00 USD Monthly	$2.25 USD	Cancelled
12/07/2016	SSD1G	$7.00 USD Monthly	$1.05 USD	Active
12/07/2016	SSD1G	$9.00 USD Monthly	$1.35 USD	Cancelled
12/03/2016	SSD2G	$13.00 USD Monthly	$1.95 USD	Active

Pretty soon, I was generating 3-figure affiliate commissions:

Current Standard Commissions

Date	Status	Sub-Affiliate ID	Commission	View Details
12-26-2016	Approved - Pending Payment	N/A	$234.00 USD	View Details
12-24-2016	Approved - Pending Payment	N/A	$18.75 USD	View Details
12-15-2016	Approved - Pending Payment	N/A	$33.50 USD	View Details

I Rank My First YouTube Videos on Google in a Matter of MINUTES

My next challenge was to learn to rank videos on Google. I studied how others have done it and modeled their strategies.

Very soon, I was able to rank my videos on Google in a matter of minutes. Check this video review I did for an upcoming product that ranked in only 6 minutes:

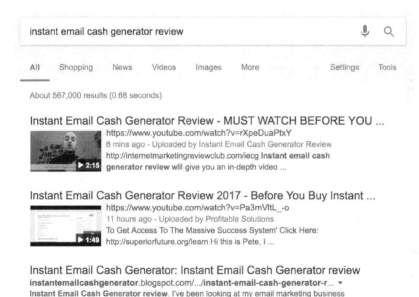

This allowed me to get a lot of extra free views by tapping into a second search engine.

My Journey Continues

This is the part of the story where my journey continues and yours begins. I have just scratched the surface of what's possible on my channels, and a lot more results and success is yet to come.

At the time of writing this book, I had made almost $500 in less than 3 months just with only a few videos, by applying the strategies I'm about to share with you.

 Since I can't keep updating this book every week, I suggest if you'd like to continue to follow me and see my current results, make sure to visit the main website (videotrafficinsider.com) and join the newsletter there for more insider YouTube tips.

Connect with me on social media, just search "Gabriel Both" on Google and you'll find my various websites and profiles.

I look forward meeting you at one of my webinars or at upcoming live events!

CHAPTER 5

Top YouTube Myths

A lot of people have preconceived ideas about what is and what isn't possible on YouTube. Let's bust some myths that you may have believed up until now.

1.   You have to go viral to be successful on YouTube

When most people hear about YouTube success, they hear about the top vloggers (video bloggers) and people who have millions of followers. Some of them had viral hits that skyrocketed them to fame.

Naturally, of course, we tend to focus on the few exceptions and then generalize that going viral is the only way to be successful on YouTube. That simply isn't true.

The fact is you must master ranking videos on YouTube. Ranking videos is about getting videos listed in the search results as close to the first position on the first page as possible. The higher it is "ranked", the more clicks and views you will get, because most people don't scroll past the first page.

You can become successful quite fast by generating a lot of free traffic and building your subscriber base rapidly.

You don't have to rely on "luck", but rather on a proven system that works, as long as you put in the effort to apply it.

2. You have to have hundreds of thousands or millions of views to make money on YouTube

The most popular way people think YouTubers make money is through the YouTube Ads. Although that may be one of their revenue streams, you do in fact need a lot of views to make decent income from this.

On YouTube, the average rate for pre-roll ads (the 30-second commercials that you must watch before seeing a video) is $7.60 per 1,000 ad views, down from $9.35 in 2012, according to TubeMogul. (NYTimes, 2014)

What most people don't know is that you actually don't need that many views to make money on YouTube. You just need a really good video, a strong call to action, and a product that this audience wants.

 Important: *Call to actions are clear directives usually added to the end of your video or sometimes in the middle to get the viewer to take action on something, such as subscribe, comment, like, or click the link in the description.*

Then you have a chance to start making sales.

Even if you just get 50 views a day on a video and get one sale every few days, you can make hundreds of dollars per month from this one video alone. I've done it myself.

3. YouTube SEO hasn't worked now since a few years

It used to be the case when all you needed to do was "stuff" your meta fields with the exact keyword you wanted to rank for and "BOOM!", you were at the top.

There are 3 terms that SEO experts often refer to. "Blackhat", "Whitehat", and "Greyhat".

Blackhat tactics are those that go against the terms of service of any platform you're using the tactics for. They are considered 'spammy' and try to take advantage or 'game' the system to get an unfair advantage over natural search results.

Whitehat tactics are those that are 100% in line with and follow the rules and best practices of the platform on which they're being used for. They require a lot more work and effort, but are sustainable in the long term.

Greyhat tactics are those that sit between Blackhat and Whitehat tactics. They try to appear as natural as possible, yet still take advantage of parts of the platform to gain an advantage.

The blackhat tactic of 'keyword stuffing' doesn't work anymore, as YouTube (and Google) has gotten smarter and more advanced, but what does work is proper whitehat YouTube SEO techniques that look natural, organic, and give YouTube more context and meaning so it understands what your video is about. We'll get into how to do that in later chapters.

4.   Viewers just want to see funny videos

Not everyone goes on to YouTube to watch funny cat videos or viral comedy clips. A lot of people go on to search "how to" videos, watch inspiring or motivational clips, or hundreds of other reasons.

The top most popular types of YouTube videos are: product reviews, how to, vlogs, gaming, comedy, shopping, memes, favorites/best of, unboxing videos, q&a, collections, and prank videos.

5. Your video needs to be Hollywood quality to be successful

No, absolutely not. Content is the most important and video quality is the icing on the cake. Besides, most of the modern smartphone cameras have excellent video quality and will do a really good job to create high quality videos.

Do you remember when you watched a movie with amazing special effects, but it totally sucked? That's proof that video quality isn't the most important - it's the content (or the story) that makes it good or bad.

6. It's expensive to promote your videos

No, you don't have to spend any money on promoting your videos. If you learn the strategies to rank your videos, then you'll save yourself boatloads of money from paid ads.

You've just got to be creative and think outside the box!

PART 2:
YOUTUBE SPECIFICS

CHAPTER **6**

Video Marketing Foundations

I n this chapter, you'll learn how to find your niche, define your target audience, and understand why finding a big problem to solve will lead to bigger money. This chapter is very important because it will increase your chances of building a successful YouTube channel.

Positioning, Niche, and Personal Branding

Before you even start on YouTube, the most important questions you need to ask yourself if you don't already have a business that you want to promote on YouTube are: **Who is your audience? And what are the main problems or pain points you're helping them solve?**

If you already have a business, you should already have an idea of the answers to these two questions. If you don't, go back and answer them.

The next concept you must understand is **positioning**. Positioning is how do you want to be viewed or "position yourself" in your market?

For example, are you going to be the #1 Weight Loss Expert for Single Moms under 30? Are you the only car engineer who can fix diesel engines with their eyes closed? Are you the best dog trainer for miniature dogs? **Be creative**… think about what "edge" you have over everyone else. How can you differentiate yourself from your competitors? What is your unique selling proposition (USP)?

When you're only starting out, it's important to have a distinct niche or topic you'll be creating content around. This has to do with a few reasons: SEO, trust, and positioning.

When you select a narrow niche, you'll be able to target longer-tail key-words (keyword phrases with 4 or more words), which generally have much less competition than shorter keywords, but still have some decent search volume.

This makes it easier for you to dominate this niche by having first page or first position rankings for those keywords. If you have a very vague or unfocused niche on your channel, YouTube will not understand very clearly what your channel is about, and your ranking ability for keywords will decrease.

One of the reasons people are going to YouTube is to find answers to questions or solutions to problems. Your video can lead them to those.

Personal branding has a lot to do with what others see you as, and how they feel about you when they come to your channel and watch your videos.

Which inspires more trust? A "jack-of-all-trades" who talks about 10 subjects or someone who is an expert in a particular niche and goes in depth about one particular subject? Of course, the latter!

 Super Tip: *If you have many very different topics you want to talk about, then it's better to create multiple channels, one for each niche.*

1) Find Your Niche

What is a niche? A niche, or niche market, is the subset of the market on which a specific product is focused. For example, a market could be "dog lovers", but a niche would be something more specific, like "golden retriever lovers".

You've probably heard at some time that you've got to "niche-down", "find a niche" or something along these lines. But why?

Let's get into the main reasons why finding a niche is so important, especially online.

As more and more businesses and people go online, the higher the competition gets. For example, on YouTube, there are probably hundreds of dog channels out there, each one trying to rank for these keywords and get subscribers.

If you come along and create another dog channel, what makes it different than the rest? Why would people subscribe to yours when there are hundreds of similar channels out there? It makes it much harder for you to rank your videos and create a profitable channel from if you don't have a niche.

Without a niche, you'll attract a general, undefined audience that may or may not relate to your videos, resonate with your message, or let alone buy your products.

When you clearly define your niche, you're literally "filtering" out people who don't relate, and focusing on the specific problems and questions this smaller group of people has. Not only does this create a sense in your viewers of "feeling understood", but people love things that are for them.

There will also be much less competition, and you can become the authority in this niche much faster by more easily ranking videos and positioning yourself as the #1 solution for the problems in this niche.

This allows you charge much higher prices and build a loyal subscriber base of raving fans.

Essential Rules for Niche Selection

When selecting your niche, you've got to look at the following criteria if you want to create a YouTube channel that you can build a profitable business around.

1)   Is your niche big enough?

This is an important question to ask, but how do you actually know how big your niche is? The answer lies in market research. You can use the following strategies to gauge the size of your niche.

Facebook Audience Insights

You can get an idea of how many people fall within a niche by using Facebook's free Audience Insights tool. You'll need to set up a free Facebook ads account first, then go to vidtr.in/fbai

From there, select "Everyone on Facebook" and select all the options that define your niche.

For example, I selected United Kingdom, Females between 25-35 years old who like "Golden Retrievers", and I got 25K-30K monthly active users. Worldwide, it has 1M-1.5M monthly active users.

Play around with the tool and you can keep narrowing down your niche to see whether this would be a good niche market to pursue.

Facebook Page and Group Sizes

Another great way to gauge niche size is to use the Facebook search function and type in your niche. Then you can filter by Pages or Groups and have a look at how many people have liked or are in these niche groups.

Again, I'll use the same example of "golden retriever" and we can see there are a lot of pages with hundreds of thousands of likes:

There are also a lot of groups with thousands of active members:

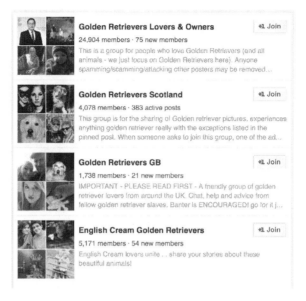

Number of Related YouTube Videos

On YouTube, you can see how many related videos there are just by searching the niche. "Golden retrievers" got me 1.01 million results and the top ranking videos have millions of views:

Size of Related YouTube Channels

The number of subscribers on a channel gives a better indication than views of how many people are interested in a niche. It was interesting to find that there weren't that many "golden retriever" dedicated niche channels. Here were a few of them, with not that many subscribers:

Golden Retriever Lovers 7 videos

Subscribe 4K

We are a community of Golden Retriever Lovers! We goldens. That's why we share the cutest golden retri videos for your enjoyment. So please subscrib...

White Oak Golden Retrievers 101 videos

Subscribe 95

Here in the foothills of the Appalachian Mountains and the Great Eastern Divide, we are home to American Red Golden Retrievers and English Cream Golden Retri...

Fritz Dog

Subscribe 21K

Fritz Dog is a YouTube channel that celebrates both unique inability to catch food and his positive, can-do attitude. While we all intently anticipat...

Golden Retriever Puppies 9 videos

Subscribe 106

Golden Retriever Puppies are, in our opinion, the cutest, most adorable puppies in the world. And whatsmore, they make the best pets. We have built this chan...

Number of Websites Listed in Google

You can get an idea of niche size by the number of websites that are on the web. By using Google's search functions, we can narrow down exactly how many website pages have been indexed for that term.

Tip: *Use the "allintitle:" operator and surround the niche keyword in double quotes to let Google know we want to search all web pages that have the full keyword phrase "golden retrievers" in the title.*

allintitle: "golden retrievers"

| All | Images | Videos | Shopping | News | More |

About 365,000 results (0.46 seconds)

Here we see around 365,000 results, which is a good number of results.

Number of Amazon Books

Chances are, if many people have written books in this niche, there is an active audience. Using Amazon search, we can see nearly 2,000 books have been published around this topic:

1-16 of 1,926 results for **Books** : **"golden retrievers"**

2) Is There Buyer Demand?

Now that you've found a niche that is large enough, it's time to check whether there is buyer demand. What this means is are people spending money in this niche? If so, how much money?

Important: *Niches with high buyer demand tend to revolve around a big problem or pain point. For example, people who are suffering from a painful disease would be willing to spend thousands of dollars on a solution.*

How do you determine whether there is buyer demand? Here are a few different ways:

Existing Products

One of the best ways to see whether people are spending money is to look whether there are existing products available on the market and if possible, see how well they are selling.

One of my favorite places to look for digital products is ClickBank.com

 Tools & Resources:

ClickBank - vidtr.in/cb

Check out ClickBank if you want a great selection of high-converting digital products to choose from in virtually every niche. You can browse their marketplace without registering.

After searching for "golden retrievers", there were 2 products that came up. The gravity score (Grav) is a number that hints at how well the product is selling, in this case it looks like these two products aren't doing too well.

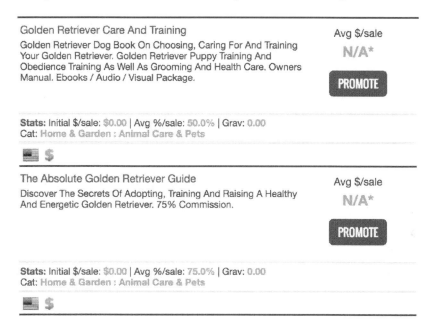

For physical products, check out Amazon, or other online ecommerce stores. Make a note at the price ranges, how many products there are, and how many categories of products exist.

Magazines

Magazines are perfect for seeing if the niche is viable, because a large source of revenue for magazine publishers come from advertisers. If advertisers don't make money on ads they buy, then they will stop spending money, simple as that.

Check out magazines.com and search your niche. See if any related magazines come up in the results.

Tools & Resources:

Magazines.com - This magazine archive has hundreds of catego-ries you can explore for magazines that relate to your niche or keyword.

PPC Advertisements and CPC

Pay per click (PPC) advertisements on Google give you clues on how profitable this niche keyword is.

If you don't see any ads when you type the phrase into Google, then chances are there's no money to be made there.

Super Tip: *If you want to find the average cost per click (CPC) for a specific keyword, you can check the CPC amounts by cre-ating a free Google Adwords account, going to their Keyword Planner tool and searching the keyword. This will give you an idea how much advertisers are willing to bid on this search phrase.*

For example, here are some of the related keyword phrases that came up, ordered from highest CPC:

dog breed info golden retriever	10 – 100	Low	£1.81
golden retriever information and ...	10 – 100	Low	£1.80
golden retriever puppies classifieds	10 – 100	High	£1.71
golden retriever mix puppies for ...	100 – 1K	Medium	£1.52
where can i adopt a golden retrie...	10 – 100	High	£1.49
rescued golden retrievers for ad...	10 – 100	Medium	£1.44

Amazon Book Sales

A great metric to check on Amazon is their "Seller Rank" score. This is calculated mostly by the number of sales the book gets overall, and for specific categories it's in. You can find this on the book details page:

Amazon Bestsellers Rank: 21,503 in Books (See Top 100 in Books)
#124 in Books > Home & Garden > Animal Care & Pets > **Dogs**

To do this, you can use a tool called KDSpy, which allows you to see more detailed results for a specific keyword, even the estimated number of sales and revenue for each book:

Keyword: **golden retriever**

Keyword Results | Keyword Analysis | Word Cloud (20) | Rank Tracking (0)

Results:	Avg. Sales Rank:	Avg. Monthly Rev:	Avg. Price:	Avg. No. Reviews:
1-20	**314,051**	**£222**	**£5.02**	**48**

#	Kindle Book Title	More	Page(s)	Price	Est. Sales	Monthly Rev.	Reviews	Sales Rank
1	Chez Stinky (An Alpine Grove Romantic Com...	T | S | C	300	£0	573	£ 0	130	1,652
2	Nigel: my family and other dogs	T | S | C	240	£9.99	337	£ 3,367	269	5,535
3	The Happy Puppy Handbook: Your Definitive ...	T | S | C	224	£9.49	78	£ 740	393	13,255
4	Address to Die For (A Maggie McDonald Mys...	T | S | C	252	£0.99	64	£ 63	2	18,959
5	The Goodness of Dogs: The Human's Guide ...	T | S | C	263	£9.99	24	£ 240	18	44,083
6	Golden Retrievers For Dummies	T | S | C	288	£10.44	1	£ 10	16	445,655
7	The Everything Golden Retriever Book: A Co...	T | S | C	304	£7.98	1	£ 8	30	322,140
8	Stray Home	T | S | C	241	£3.25	1	£ 3	13	105,032
9	My Life In His Paws: The Story of Ted and Ho...	T | S | C	288	£9.99	1	£ 10	59	148,873
10	Golden Retriever Training: Breed Specific Pu...	T | S | C	57	£2.16	1	£ 2	15	209,968
11	Golden Retriever Training | Dog Training with...	T | S | C	237	£3.01	1	£ 3	4	155,450
12	Your Golden Retriever Puppy Month by Month	T | S | C	370	£7.99	1	£ 8	7	169,786
13	Chasing Chance (Angel Paws)	T | S | C	26	£0.99	1	£ 1	1	152,214
14	Skunks Smell Splendid: Adventures of a Gold...	T | S | C	13	£0	0	£ 0	0	0
15	Golden Retriever Handbook: The Definitive G...	T | S | C	45	£2.61	0	£ 0	1	788,813
16	Golden Retriever Training: Principles and Pra...	T | S | C	31	£1.28	0	£ 0	0	755,080
17	Golden Retriever: A Comprehensive Guide to...	T | S | C	174	£9.49	0	£ 0	2	940,374
18	Golden Retriever	T | S | C	9	£2.46	0	£ 0	0	0
19	Draw 50 Dogs: The Step-by-Step Way to Dra...	T | S | C	64	£5.92	0	£ 0	4	562,283
20	The Golden Retriever: A Complete and Comp...	T | S | C	59	£2.3	0	£ 0	3	1,441,871

What does this have to do with YouTube? Well, if the book sales are not that great on Amazon, then chances are people who watch your videos and subscribe to your channel on YouTube will have similar spending patterns.

 **Tools & Resources:**

KDSpy - vidtr.in/kdspy

This software allows you to see how profitable a certain category or keyword phrase is on Amazon. This is helpful to gauge how much an audience is spending in a given niche.

3) Are there evergreen products you can promote?

If you plan to promote any type of product, then this is an important question you need to ask yourself.

You'll want to have a large selection of products you can offer on a website, through an affiliate link, or other platform, otherwise, you'll run dry really fast and have limited income potential.

Also, make sure they are "Evergreen", meaning they stand the test of time and aren't products that are time-bound or depend on trends that can disappear quickly.

Action Step: *If this is something you'd like to start, check out places like ClickBank.com, JVZoo.com, Avangate, Commission Junction, Rakuten, and Amazon.com for products you could promote that relate to your niche. A good minimum target number is 50-100+ products.*

Tools & Resources:

JVZoo - vidtr.in/jvz

This is another great platform for finding digital products and affiliate offers to promote.

Tools & Resources:

Avangate - vidtr.in/agt

This platform has a wide range of affiliate programs you can choose from and sign up to, so register and then browse the selection - see if anything fits your niche.

Tools & Resources:

Commission Junction - vidtr.in/cj

Another solid affiliate network with hundreds of programs to sign up to. I definitely recommend getting an account with them, as there are a lot of great affiliate programs listed on here.

Tools & Resources:

Rakuten Affiliate Network - vidtr.in/rktn

Similar to the previous two, Rakuten is another large affiliate network with a lot of programs to choose from.

Tools & Resources:

Amazon Associates - vidtr.in/amzn

If you want to promote Amazon books or any product on the site, then sign up to become an associate so you can start earning a commission on things your recommend.

The three biggest and best product niche categories are:

- Making money
- Health and wellness
- Love, relationships, and dating

These will always be around as long as humans are alive, so see whether you can find a niche in one of these categories.

4) Are you passionate about it?

Finally, if your niche passed the previous three criteria, then you'll need to ask yourself whether you're passionate or have some interest in the niche you're selecting.

If the answer is no, then forget it. You must love it enough to be able to talk about it on end, because you'll be creating lots of video content around it, and investing your time, energy, and money into it. Challenges will come up that will test your patience and stamina. Only your passion will be able to keep you going through them.

Also, people will be able to sense whether you're passionate about the topics you talk about. They will be able to hear it in your voice, see it in your face, and feel it in your message. Passion is contagious and you will attract the right audience if you love the niche you're in.

Guaranteed, if you are genuinely excited about a product, then you'll make others feel excited about it too and you'll make many more sales than if you weren't.

2) Define Your Audience

Knowing your audience is key to be able to successfully communicate a marketing message. To be able to serve someone, you first need to know them and exactly what their needs are. Therefore, it's very important to first clearly define your audience so you can effectively craft your marketing message specifically for them.

Ask yourself: if you were to sit in a café at a table of two, who would your ideal subscriber, customer, or client be?

In order to tailor your message to the right people, you first need to know whom you're talking to.

You've already decided your niche, so now you must define the audience you will serve within this niche.

The common mistake most people make is trying to be everything to everybody. That will only result in reaching nobody.

The best exercise you can do to define your audience is to create an ideal "customer avatar". This will be the person who will be sitting across from you in the imagined café that you'll be talking to.

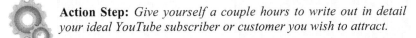 **Action Step:** *Give yourself a couple hours to write out in detail your ideal YouTube subscriber or customer you wish to attract.*

Give them a full name. Are they male or female? How old are they? How much do they earn? What do they do for a living? Where do they live? What are their hopes, dreams, and desires? What are their pains, frustrations, worries, and problems? What are their other interests?

Go into as much detail as you can and aim for at least 2-3 pages.

The purpose for doing this is so whenever you are creating your videos, you imagine yourself speaking to this person. This will attract viewers and subscribers to your channel who are similar to this ideal customer/subscriber avatar.

Of course, you'll have people who don't fit the description, and that's OK, but the majority of your core following will be very close to this avatar.

They will feel as if you are talking to them one-to-one, and will feel you understand their problems and needs. This builds a lot of trust and loyalty, which is essential for any brand and business.

3) Solve a Big Problem

Understand that people spend only as much money proportionally as the problem they are trying to solve. A bigger problem will command a bigger price and lead to larger sales.

Problems are subjective, depending on how valuable the solution is to the person. For example, if you're helping people find a natural remedy for sore throat, that's a relatively small problem and people wouldn't spend hundreds or thousands of dollars to find a solution.

On the other hand, if you're helping professional athletes accelerate their recovery from a broken bone, where their career is at stake, then that's a much bigger problem and they would pay a lot of money for an effective solution.

 Important: *My advice is if you want to make the most money on YouTube is to choose a niche with a big problem. Ask yourself: If I were my ideal audience, would I do everything I could and spend a lot of money finding a solution to this?*

If the answer is yes, then it's a big problem, which means big money.

CHAPTER 7

Create Your YouTube Channel

N ow that you've decided on your niche and defined your target audience, it's finally time to create and setup your YouTube channel. I'll go step by step through everything you will need to consider and do to set it up properly.

1)   Create a Google account

If you don't already have a Google account, then you can set one up for free by going to google.com and entering your relevant info. You'll need a mobile number to activate it.

2)   Name your default account channel

Once you've created your Google account, simply go to youtube.com. When you first sign in and create a channel, you'll be asked for your name as your channel name. This will be your default account channel and you don't have to use it.

3)   Create a new brand channel

Once you have your account channel in place, you can create additional channels, which are known as brand channels, and you can name these anything you want. To add a new brand channel, simply go to your Account Settings page and click on "See all my channels or create a new channel", then "+ Create a new channel".

4) Configure your channel settings

- Under Creator Studio → Channel → Status and features, I recommend you verify your channel so you can unlock additional useful features like being able to upload videos longer than 15 minutes, adding custom thumbnails, and so on…
- Under "Upload Defaults" select your default category for your videos and whether you want to upload them as private, unlisted or public. I prefer private, and then publishing them when I'm ready.
- Under "Branding", you can add a watermark, which can be your logo and will show up in the bottom right corner of all your videos. When viewers hover over it, they will be able to subscribe to your channel.
- Finally, under "Advanced", you can select your country, and add your channel keywords. You can also link your channel with Google AdWords if you wish to do paid YouTube ads in the future.

5) Brand your channel

Go back to your channel homepage and you can now add a channel description. Make sure to include some of your main keywords in there for SEO. If you click on the gear icon, select "Customize the layout of your channel", which allows you to add links and create sections. Simply select the content you want to feature, and the layout style.

6)   Create your banner and profile image

It's time now to create your channel art and icon. If you're not a graphic designer, then I recommending going on Fiverr.com and having it designed there for $5-$15.

 Tools & Resources:

Fiverr - vidtr.in/fiverr

You can outsource pretty much anything on here, but you'll need to do some research to find high quality sellers with good ratings and portfolios.

 If you do choose to design it yourself, then for the banner art, you'll need dimensions of 2560 x 1440. You can download the template here: vidtr.in/bannerart.

Add your channel name, tagline, and logo as well as some images that would relate to your audience.

For the banner icon, I recommend dimensions of 800 x 800 and you can put your profile image, or your logo here. You will be adding this on your Google account page, so it may take a few hours to show up on your YouTube channel.

7)   Create your featured video

On your channel homepage, you can also have a featured video. This can be an intro video telling your new viewers what this channel is about, who it's for, and the benefits of becoming a subscriber. You can also just tell your story, as it will help them connect with you. You can select your featured video here: Creator Studio → Channel → Featured content.

Great, so you've set up your channel and you're excited to get started. The next important step in the process is Keyword Research.

CHAPTER **8**

Effective Keyword Research

K eyword research is the market research stage of the process where you look at what your audience is searching for on YouTube or Google. The more searches a keyword has, the more demand and larger the audience.

To do keyword research effectively, you'll learn why keyword research is important, the difference between YouTube and Google keywords, how to find high search volume keywords with low competition and high profitability, as well as find out the top keyword research tools that you can use to do your research.

What is a Keyword?

When I talk about a keyword, what I mean is a phrase of one or more words that represent what people are typing into YouTube or Google to search for something. I may refer to it as "search term", "search phrase", "keyword phrase", "keywords", "key terms", or something similar.

You might see me talking about "long tail keywords". These are simply keywords that contain 4 or more words. Long tail keywords tend to have much less searches, but also less competition and will usually be more specific, so you can see more clearly what the intent of the searcher is.

Why Do Keyword Research?

Most people on YouTube create content, then upload it and pray that people will find it. No wonder most of them don't find success. A few may have a video go viral, but that's pure luck. Instead, follow an effective system that's proven to work.

Fewer people than the ones who just upload a video without thought, will create a video, and then try to optimize that video around a specific keyword, hoping that it will rank. This is still the wrong way of doing things. They have the order of the process reversed. It should be first find a keyword, then create and optimize a video around that keyword.

The very few search marketers who get high rankings and lots of free traffic over and over again start first with finding a keyword that people are actually searching for.

 Important: *Good marketers always start by looking at market demand and then give the audience exactly what they want.*

There's no point creating a video on a topic that 10 people a month are searching for, unless it is proven to be super profitable.

 Tip: *It's far better to find a keyword with low competition and decent search volume, and then create a video exactly around that. This is the strategy you need to follow if you want to rank high and get lots of free traffic.*

YouTube Keywords

Since YouTube doesn't have its own keyword research tool like Google does, finding keywords to rank on YouTube is a bit more of a guessing game, however there is one cool feature that will show you exactly what people are search for.

If you go to the YouTube search bar and start typing, you'll start seeing suggested searches drop down from field. These suggested searches reflect exactly what searches are popular on YouTube right now. The higher up in the list the search phrase is, the more potential searches it has.

Tip: *I usually choose one of the top 3 suggested phrases for my main video keyword and go for long tail keywords with at least 5+ words.*

The only 3rd party keyword research tool I know of that is geared towards YouTube specifically is YTCockpit.

Tools & Resources:

YTCockpit - vidtr.in/ytc

This tool enables you to search keywords on YouTube and find profitable keyword ideas that will get you high-quality traffic. You can look at competition, and other key metrics to decide whether this keyword is worth creating a video around. The Pro version also has the ability to track keyword positions.

I also use VidIQ to check for YouTube keyword competition and potential search volume.

Tools & Resources:

VidIQ - vidtr.in/viq

This free Google Chrome plugin helps you to rank your YouTube videos higher by providing suggestions for optimizing your videos. It will suggest tags, and also give you a keyword competition score and potential traffic you could expect. It also gives you an SEO score and VidIQ score for popularity/engagement. One of the features I love is it automatically reveals the tags for a video and shows how high the video is ranking for each tag.

Google Video Keywords

Google will only rank certain types of videos in their search engine.

If you're looking to rank your videos on Google, then you'll need to see if the keyword is a "video keyword", meaning are there any videos already ranked on Google for this keyword.

Some of the most common types of video keywords are:

- How-to keywords ("How to do 100 pushups")
- Reviews ("iPhone 7 review")
- Tutorials ("Setting up a Wordpress site")
- Anything fitness or sports related ("Taekwondo fitness")
- Funny videos ("Funny cats")
- Local videos ("Emergency plumber [location]")

 Tip: *The best way to find out if a keyword is a video keyword is to just type into Google and see whether there are any existing videos there. If not, then there are two options: either nobody has tried ranking for it, or it's not a video keyword.*

Keyword Volume

Keyword volume is the measurement of how many searches per month a specific keyword phrase has. The higher the number, the more estimated number of searches it has.

Unfortunately, YouTube doesn't have a way to check how many users are searching for a particular keyword per month, but I'll show you a way you can estimate it using Google's keyword tool.

Keyword Research Tools

As mentioned previously, use the YouTube autosuggestion feature to find keywords for best possible YouTube ranking.

To gauge how many searches YouTube could be getting for a certain keyword, or if you choose to rank your video on Google and see how many searches per month there are, use the Google Keyword Planner tool.

 Tools & Resources:

Google Keyword Planner - vidtr.in/gkp

A free tool by Google to allow you to research keywords that people are searching for in Google and also let you gauge how many could be searching for that term on YouTube.

You'll need to sign up for free with your Google account to adwords.google.com and then go to Tools → Keyword Planner.

From there, you can type in your keyword and get a list of related keyword phrases, with the estimated number of monthly searches it has.

Since YouTube is the world's second largest search engine, the chances that somebody will search the same Google keyword on YouTube is quite high.

Therefore, we can get a general idea of a keyword search volume on YouTube. Let's say a keyword has 1,000 monthly searches on Google, then at least a percentage of those people could also be searching on YouTube.

The only way to find out for sure is to check whether the keyword appears in the YouTube autosuggestions or actually ranks for the keyword in the first few positions of the first page and see how many views you get.

Recently, Google has limited the data in their Keyword Planner to number ranges, which are not specific, so use a tool called KWFinder, which gives more exact search volume.

Tools & Resources:

KWFinder - vidtr.in/kwfinder

A great all-round keyword research tool. Allows you to see exact search volumes for keywords unlike the limited ranges in Keyword Planner. It also has a very pretty and intuitive interface and calculates the keyword competitiveness score to give you an idea how easy it would be to rank for that keyword in Google. There's a free version, but it's limited to only a few keyword lookups per day.

If you want a keyword research tool with more keyword allowance and is easier to use for bulk sets of keywords, then I suggest using Long Tail Platinum.

Tools & Resources:

Long Tail Platinum - vidtr.in/ltp

It used to be only a desktop app, but recently they've switched to the cloud, making it much faster and more reliable. It also has an exact search volumes and keyword competitiveness scores. It has a 7-day $1 trial you can test out.

If the previous two keyword research tools don't appeal to you, then have a look at SECockpit. It also has a lot of quality features you'd expect in a decent keyword research tool worth its salt.

Tools & Resources:

SECockpit - vidtr.in/sec

This software is made by the same company as YTCockpit, but this one is more geared toward Google SEO. It has the latest features, including exact monthly searches, keyword competitiveness, filtering, and even a mobile app. The Pro version includes keyword tracking as well.

Keyword Profitability

When you're ranking videos on YouTube to grow your business, you want to make sure that the keywords you're ranking for have some commercial viability, meaning: are they profitable?

By now, you should have already selected a profitable niche, but now we are going to go into finer detail and look at specific keyword income potential.

What you need to do is use the free Google Keyword Planner tool again, but this time you'll be looking at the average CPC (cost per click) bid value. This is on average how many advertisers on the Google AdWords platform are paying per click to their ads that show up in the Google search results.

Advertisers will only pay for ads if they bring them a return on their investment, meaning they are making sales. They will only spend a lot of money per click if they are making a lot of money from advertising for that keyword.

Therefore, by looking at the value, we can get an idea how valuable a keyword is on Google. Again, chances are if people are searching for it on Google and purchasing things, then they probably are searching on it in YouTube and would also purchase something if the video leads to a product or service.

Buyer Keywords

Behind every keyword is an intention. By analyzing the words in the keyword phrase, we can get an idea of where people are in the sales process.

Action Step: *Ask yourself: Are they just searching to look around? Are they interested in a product already and are comparing types or looking for the best prices? Are they searching for reviews to see if it's any good? Or are they ready to buy now?*

Here are some of the most common buyer keyword examples:

- [brand] [product] review
- [product 1] vs [product 2]
- top/best [product]
- cheapest [product]
- buy [product] online
- [product] coupons/discounts/deals

A good rule of thumb is asking yourself: **What is the intention behind the keyword phrase?**

Tip: *Keep a "keyword swipe file". As you do your keyword research, make sure you have an Excel or Google Sheets spreadsheet to store your top keywords in, with columns for search volume, CPC, competition, and notes. You'll be referring back to this file whenever you want to create another video to rank.*

CHAPTER 9

Create Your Videos

N ow that you have your keywords ready, it's time to create your videos. But before you grab your camera and start shooting videos randomly, there are a few important things you need to know first so you can create the most engaging videos for maximum results.

What information is important to put into a YouTube video?

The content you create in your YouTube video must reflect your audience's needs. People go on YouTube for 3 primary reasons - to be:

1)   Educated
2)   Entertained
3)   Motivated

Ideally, your video should do all three, but it's best to focus on your strengths and choose a style that best suits you.

The information or content you add to the video needs to cater to what your audience likes. That's why first defining and then getting to know your audience is very important, so you can "target" your message so they feel like you understand and know them.

If your video is created to educate, then it's more about facts, answers to questions, solutions to problems, keeping them up to date with the latest news, and other useful and valuable information. You can do market research in a variety of different ways to see what your audience would find valuable. Here are some to get you started:

- **Facebook Audience Insights** (vidtr.in/fbai) – You'll need a free Facebook Ads account, and then you can use this to define your audience by location, age range, gender, and more and see what pages they like, what interests them, which kind of profession they are in, and much more...

- **Quora.com** – This website is a goldmine! It's basically a place where people go to ask and answer questions in different niches. You can select the niches or interests and then browse all the different questions there are. You can then answer these questions in video form and upload to YouTube.

- **Reddit.com** – This is a really great platform again to connect and engage with your audience in a community where you can see what questions they have and discover problems they're experiencing that you can solve.

- **Twitter Search** – In Twitter, you can search all tweets on the platforms. Not many people have heard of it or used it, but it's an excellent way to "get into the minds" of your audience. If you go to twitter.com/search-home, you can enter the keywords it should search for. Add a "?" and add a few operators to filter out tweets with links (-http –https).

- **Amazon Book Reviews** – People will tell you what they think and what they want or didn't find in a book in the reviews. Choose a popular book in your niche and dive into the reviews section. Look for reviews between 2 and 4 stars as these contain a lot of suggestions and reveal the gaps and weak points of the book that you could cover in your YouTube video. Keep a document or "swipe file" where you copy and paste these reviews in that you could later refer to when you're looking to create a new video on your channel.

- **Google Trends** – If you want to ride the wave of the latest news, topics, or trends, then use Google Trends to see what media is getting the most attention and searches that you could take advantage of.

 Tools & Resources:

Google Trends - vidtr.in/gtrends

Find out what is trending and what people are searching for right now. If you create a video around it, chances are it could get a lot of exposure and views.

- **Buzz Sumo** – This is a really awesome tool where you can see the latest viral and trending articles that you could model into a video.

 Tools & Resources:

Buzz Sumo - vidtr.in/buzz

This tool is a goldmine of ideas for article headlines that have went viral in the past. If you create a video version of one of them, it increases the chance of it going viral. Use the powerful search function to find articles relating to your niche.

Want to entertain or motivate?

If your video is mostly designed to **entertain**, then it's important to have a theme in mind; something that your audience can relate to and humor that fits them as well. If you need ideas for funny videos, then model the best out there by looking at funny trending videos on YouTube, Facebook, Instagram, etc. Create something similar, and put your twist on it!

Finally, if you're looking to primarily **motivate**, then you'll need to know what kind of action you want your viewer to take. Give them all the benefits and reasons why they should take action, and why they should do it NOW, rather than later!

The more you infuse it with emotion, the more likely they will act. Humans are driven by two primary things: pain and pleasure. Pain usually is more motivating than pleasure, so try to focus on giving reasons why if they don't take action, they will experience some sort of pain. When you combine both pain and pleasure, it creates an even more powerful force. Behavioral psychology suggests that most people are driven by emotion first and then justify their actions with logic afterwards.

Telling stories are a good way to both engage your viewer and add emotion. It's been said that "stories sell, facts tell", so if you can, weave your information into a story.

Super Tip: *The ideal video combines all three styles together – teach them something valuable while you entertain your audience and at the same time, motivate them to take action at the end so they see positive results in their own life. That is a sure-fire winner!*

Here are some other content ideas that you could use:

•   **Book summaries** – These days, people don't have much time. If you can extract the best parts and top tips from the latest books, people will love that because you'll be saving them time.

- **Interviews** – In your niche, contact experts and ask them if you can interview them. You can do it in person or over Skype. Have a list of interesting questions that your audience would ask or you would find interesting or valuable to learn. Make sure you ask their permission if you can use the video on your channel, in a book, or other product you may use it in.

- **Lists** – Having a video about "Top 10..." or "20 Best..." is valuable because most people don't want to go through the effort of filtering through things themselves to find the best things. Usually, the larger the lists, the better, but don't make the video too long. Better to break it down into subcategories. If you can create these lists, you'll have viewers flock to your video in droves.

- **Reviews** – If you've used a product, service, or read a good book recently that you highly recommend, then create a video review! People are skeptical and want to see if something is any good before they buy. If you can be honest with your review, you'll establish trust with your audience.

Do you have to be in front of a camera?

No, if you absolutely don't want to be in front of a camera, that's fine - you still have a few options. But before I go into these, you'll be missing out on a few really good benefits that you get only with you being on camera:

- **People can connect with you better and tend to trust you more when they see a real person behind the screen**. We are hardwired to connect with faces. You can read a lot behind the words in the body language and in the eyes and face, so you can more easily discern if someone's being genuine or is hiding something.

86

- **You will be able to better brand yourself as an expert and build an image that can make you millions over time** if done right. Remember, when you do personal branding right, people will pay you for who you ARE, and not so much for what you DO. Then you can charge whatever price you want and your clients will pay it.

If you're still not convinced, fine - maybe you'll have the courage to give it a good shot in the future, but for now, here are a few ways you can create a video **without** being in front of the camera:

- **Screencast recordings** – This is great if you're showing how to use an application or reviewing a piece of software on your computer. Your computer screen is recorded in real time and you can record your voice along with it to add content. Some great tools are ScreenFlow for Mac and Camtasia for Windows. Most programs allow you to later edit it, zoom in, add mouse highlights, arrows, etc.

Tools & Resources:

Camtasia (PC/Mac) - vidtr.in/ctsa

Definitely one of the top screencasting tools on the market with a lot of superb features and also a stand-alone video editor build in. Highly recommended.

Tools & Resources:

ScreenFlow (Mac) - vidtr.in/sf

I have been using this program for many years and I love it. It has a great balance of features and simplicity and also has a stand-alone video editor built in that I use to edit non-screencast videos as well.

- **Powerpoint slides** – If you prefer to have a presentation and record it as you go through slide-by-slide, then this format will allow you to add text, images, and whatever else you want. I use this to create video modules or cover topics that need more technical explanation and diagrams. You can use Microsoft Powerpoint, Google Slides, or similar to create the slides, then use a screencast recording program to record the screen along with your voice.

- **VSLs** – Short for Video Sales Letters, these are similar to powerpoint slides in that you would use the same programs, but the style is different. It's basically a sales letter in the form of a video. The structure and flow is important so you would usually split the text into 1 or 2 lines per slide in the center.

 Tools & Resources:

EasyVSL - vidtr.in/evsl

If you're looking to create video sales letters really quickly, then this is for you. I've used it and love how quickly I can just paste my VSL text, split it up, choose my background font style, and then add my voice-over or use a pre-recorded one and sync it up. Highly recommended.

- **Animations** – If you have an animation program or pre-created animations that you cut together, these can increase video engagement and view time. There are lots of free and paid animation programs out there. Some are whiteboard animations, others might be cartoon style, some might be kinetic text (moving stylized   text).

Tools & Resources:

VideoMakerFx (PC/Mac) - vidtr.in/vmfx

If you're looking for a nice selection of animation templates, then this software will fit your needs. It has whiteboard videos, explainer videos, kinetic typography, VSLs, presentations, photo slideshows, logo openers, and much more. Definitely have a look at their demos.

Tools & Resources:

Viddyoze - vidtr.in/voze

This has an amazing selection of animated video animations, which include intros, outros, social media call to actions, and much, much more. Well worth it!

Tools & Resources:

Adobe After Effects (PC/Mac) - vidtr.in/aae

If you're more advanced and want to create your own animations, then the Adobe After Effects program will do the job. There is definitely a learning curve, so don't get it unless you really want to master it and use it properly.

Tools & Resources:

Powtoon - vidtr.in/pwt

This website allows you to create animated videos

and presentations for free. It's mostly geared toward explainer videos.

Tools & Resources:

Moovly - vidtr.in/mvly

This is very similar to Powtoon - just another option if you want to have some more choice.

Tools & Resources:

Videoscribe (PC/Mac) - vidtr.in/vsc

This software allows you to easily create stunning, HD whiteboard-style animation videos without any design knowledge or technical knowhow. It's pretty awesome and also has a huge library of whiteboard images to choose from.

- **Webinar recordings** – If you're doing a live webinar, you can usually record it so you can later upload it to YouTube for future viewing. Most webinars are in the form of a powerpoint document. Some great webinar tools are GoToWebinar and Easy-Webinar.

Can you make a YouTube video without a "video"?

Yes, you can, however, it's best to have an actual motion "video" because it's more engaging and holds the attention of the viewer longer.

The exception of course is music or podcasts, because the audio is the most important part, so if you're an artist, podcaster, or have rights to some audio, then simply a high resolution still photo of the song or album cover will do.

You will still need to use a video-editing program to add the still image with the audio to compile the video file for upload.

Effective Video Structure

Your video structure will determine how engaging your video will be, how much of the video your viewers will watch, and how many will click on your link afterwards.

 Super Tip: *A very simple but effective video structure has three parts, and the recommended total length is 2-3 minutes:*

1. *Grab attention*

2. *Add value*

3. *Call to action*

1) Grab attention - People's attention spans are short. You need to "hook" them in with a powerful benefit or curiosity-based headline.

Tell them the pain they will avoid if they watch the video to the end and the results they can expect to get if they apply the information you will share with them.

This is also when you introduce yourself briefly and qualify yourself, so it answers the hidden question "why should I listen to you?".

2) Add value - The body of the video is all about adding value and giving the audience what you promised in the beginning. It doesn't have to be a lot.

One valuable tip is fine, but make sure it's not common knowledge that someone already knows or can easily find online.

3) Call to action - This is the final part of the video where you tell them if they want to learn more, then click on the link below in the description.

It's important that this part is filled with specific benefits and let them know exactly what they will get and exactly what they need to do to get it. For example:

"If you want to learn the simple 5 step process on how I ranked a YouTube video on Google in 3 minutes, then click on the link below in the description and you'll land on a page where can enter your details to get instant access to the PDF. Ranking videos on Google can get you thousands of free views per month and lead to tons of extra sales that can grow your business. Click on the link below, and I'll see you there."

Equipment Required

Depending on what type of video you're creating, you'll need different equipment.

 Tools & Resources: *If you're just doing screencasts or animations, then all you need is a good quality microphone for speech voiceovers. The Blue Microphones Yeti or Snowball mic is a good choice and connects with USB.*

If cinema-level quality is what you're after, then you'll need a high-end prosumer camcorder, preferably with 4K, optical image stabilization and 10-20x optical zoom.

Check out the Panasonic and Canon models, they have some great options. You'll also need a high quality tripod that is light but durable and has a 2-way fluid head for smooth panning and tilting.

Tools & Resources: *I would also recommend getting a stand alone audio recorder (like ones from Tascam) plus a clip-on lapel mic, so you can record your voice if you're far away from the camera. Get a decent sized SD card so you don't have to worry about it filling up too fast.*

For most YouTubers, a modern smartphone with HD video recording and a decent lens will do the job. The latest iPhones usually have really good image quality. If you're more leaning towards Android, then Google Pixel phone or some of the latest Samsung or LG phones will do just fine.

You may also want to look at the GoPro range of cameras if you do a lot of action or outdoor videos. See if you need any equipment like selfie sticks or clips for different gear.

If you're doing a lot of indoor filming, then getting a set of softbox or video studio lights will greatly enhance the quality of your videos. If you're into green screen, then you can also get a whole kit that includes everything you need, including lights.

Tools & Resources:

Filming from the air can be done with the latest drones - check out Dji.com, GoPro.com and Parrot.com for the latest models.

If you're outsourcing your videos, then you obviously don't need any equipment.

Create Stunning Thumbnails

It always surprises me how few YouTube videos have decent thumbnails. Most videos either have an automatically generated thumbnail or if they do have one, the design is completely unappealing or boring.

This is amazing news for you! Why? Because there is a lot of opportunity for you to make your videos stand out and grab the attention of prospective viewers.

 Important: *Remember, the goal of a thumbnail is to grab attention and get the user to click on your video. The more attention your thumbnail commands, the higher your click-through rate will be!*

To do that, there are a few things you need to keep in mind.

First, type in the keyword you want to rank for in YouTube and have a look at the competition. What kind of colors, sizes of fonts, and background images are they using? How can you be different and stand out?

Here are a few guidelines I recommend following when creating your video thumbnails:

- Use bright, bold colors that are the opposite of the majority of the other videos.
- Use big, bold, bright text (with your main keyword) that "pops out" and is easy to read.
- Use bright, eye-grabbing patterns that steer the eyes to a specific point on the thumbnail.
- Ideally, have a face in there with an interesting or strong expression to evoke emotion, as people are hardwired to connect with faces.

 Super Tip: *If you want to design your own thumbnail, then I recommend using Canva.com or Pixlr.com and choosing a resolution of 1280 x 720 pixels.*

Tools & Resources:

Canva - vidtr.in/canva

This is a really great tool for creating YouTube thumbnails quickly and easily, straight from your web browser. It has a lot of free templates, backgrounds, and fonts to choose from, but you can also upload your own images too.

Tools & Resources:

Pixlr - vidtr.in/pixlr

Another alternative to Canva, this is more of a free-form image editor that allows more flexibility to create your thumbnails.

I use Pixabay.com for sourcing high quality images.

Tools & Resources:

Pixabay.com - vidtr.in/pxby

For copyright-free public domain images, I use this website to source my backgrounds for my YouTube thumbnails. It has a really good selection and a lot of high quality images to choose from.

Alternatively, you can outsource your thumbnail on Fiverr.com for $5 or if you are doing a lot of videos, hire a graphic designer on Upwork.com, Freelancer.com or People Per Hour. This will save you a lot of time and hassle over the long term.

Tools & Resources:

Upwork - vidtr.in/upwk

If you want more flexibility or want to hire an outsourcer for a more longer-term or dedicated jobs, then this platform is awesome. I've been using it for many years and I've found a lot of talent on here for really good prices.

Tools & Resources:

Freelancer - vidtr.in/flcr

Another alternative to Upwork if you prefer a different platform. I haven't used it much, but it's definitely highly rated.

Tools & Resources:

People Per Hour - vidtr.in/pph

Again, a different option to check out if you didn't like Upwork or Freelancer.

Edit Your Videos

Once you've created your video, you most likely will need to edit it or at least trim the beginning and ending.

The video editing software you use will vary based on what operating system you have, what types of videos you're creating and what your budget is.

If you're doing screencasts, then I recommend using Camtasia (PC/Mac) or ScreenFlow (Mac). Both of these programs have stand-alone editing capabilities.

For more professional videos, Adobe Premiere (PC/Mac) or Final Cut Pro (Mac) is a great choice.

Tools & Resources:

Adobe Premiere (PC/Mac) - vidtr.in/aprm

A professional-level editing suite; it may have too many features for you if you're just looking for a simple editing program, but it's great if you're doing more professional editing and want all the advanced features.

Tools & Resources:

Final Cut Pro (Mac) - vidtr.in/fcp

If you use a Mac, then this should be your go-to editor for professional video editing with all the features you'll ever need.

There are also a lot of other video editing programs out there, which you can research.

If you prefer to save time and do most of your filming on your smartphone, there are a lot of video editing apps available in the App Store or Google Play Store.

Important: *Editing your video will allow you to add intros, cut out silences, remove mistakes, adjust audio levels, layer other videos on top, add photos, add text, add transitions, and much more.*

If you are not yet skilled in editing videos, it's not that hard to learn. Just start playing around and you'll learn by trial and error, or you can get a video-editing course on Udemy.com that goes into specific software and how to use it.

Tools & Resources:

Udemy.com - This is the world's biggest platform for buying and selling video courses. It's perfect for learning new skills, or if you have a skill to share, start earning passive income by becoming an instructor and creating your own courses.

Tip: *If you don't want to touch video editing at all, then find a skilled video editor on Fiverr.com or Upwork.com and hire them to edit your videos. This will definitely save you a lot of time and cut out work you don't enjoy. You'll want the video to be in at least HD 720p, but preferably in HD 1080p or 4K quality.*

Outsource Your Videos

If all you want to focus on 100% is the making money part of YouTube and you don't want to create your own videos, then you can always outsource them.

You can get pretty much any type of video created for you. For example, on Fiverr.com you can find someone to write your video script, then find an actor to film the script, then hire a video editor to edit it all together, and finally have someone upload it to your channel and add all the meta tags and details.

You can find whiteboard animation videos, kinetic typography videos, explainer videos, video sales letters, and much more…

Super Tip: *If budget is an issue, then first do it yourself and once you start generating income on YouTube and building capital, then you can free up more of your time by outsourcing the parts you don't enjoy. This will allow you to scale up your output and lead to greater results.*

CHAPTER 10

YouTube SEO

T his is arguably one of the most powerful chapters of this whole book, showing you exactly how you can best optimize your videos for highest search rankings. You'll learn all the steps you need to take from uploading your videos, to publishing and boosting your video. You'll also learn all the YouTube ranking factors that affect your rankings.

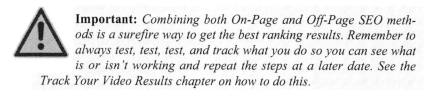 **Important:** *Combining both On-Page and Off-Page SEO methods is a surefire way to get the best ranking results. Remember to always test, test, test, and track what you do so you can see what is or isn't working and repeat the steps at a later date. See the Track Your Video Results chapter on how to do this.*

Upload Your Videos

After editing your video, it's time to upload it to YouTube. But before you upload it, there are a few things you must do to optimize it.

1)   Prepare Your Video

YouTube and Google both look at the filenames and file meta data to check for context and keywords. Therefore, to optimize ranking ability, you'll need to get it ready before you upload.

2) Filenames and Meta

What you need to do is set the name of the video and thumbnail image file the keyword phrase. This will give YouTube a clearer idea about what your video is about.

Then, depending on the operating system you're using, you can edit the video file properties and add meta tags. I add the main keyword in there as well, both for the video and the thumbnail.

3) Upload as Private

 Tip: *I highly recommend uploading your video as private so you can add all your video details and get everything ready to go before you publish it. Once you publish it, you have a limited window of time where YouTube will gauge the number of views and interaction within the first few hours to 24 hours.*

YouTube Video Ranking Factors

In this section, you'll learn about all the different factors that affect your video ranking and the ones that YouTube looks for when it is determining how high it should rank your video for a certain keyword.

I want to credit Stoica for a similar diagram he shared with me in one of his newsletter emails about all the different factors that YouTube looks for when ranking a video.

I've adapted and re-created the diagram for a more modern look, and you can also view it online, share it on social media, or even embed it on your blog or website.

 You can download the full diagram here: vidtr.in/factors

Title, Tags, Description – These are the "on-page" SEO factors, or the text that goes with the video that gives context and allows YouTube to determine what the video is about. Along with this is the video filename, captions (aka closed captions or cc), annotations, outgoing links, and content uniqueness (text that is unique and not copy-pasted from elsewhere).

Number of Views – YouTube looks at the number of views on both your video, your channel, and overall views across all of your videos. It also takes into account the source of the views, how many initial views the video gets within the first 24-48 hours, and very importantly, the view retention. View retention means how long out of the total length of the video does the viewer watch? There are two types of view retention: relative retention and absolute retention.

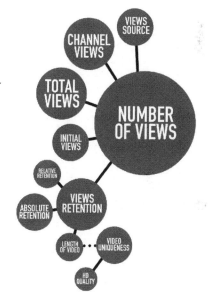

Relative retention is when YouTube compares the retention rate to similar length videos. Absolute retention is how long you keep your viewers engaged on your specific video and whether there any points in the video that keep them engaged longer than normal.

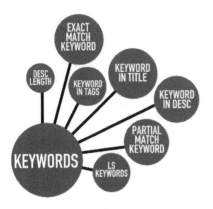

Keywords – This factor includes the length of the description, using the exact match of the keyword phrase, the keyword in the title, description and tags, and also having some secondary similar keywords sprinkled in there.

Channel – The channel name, number of subscribers, total number of videos, age of the channel, and the SEO in the channel description and tags all play a role in how well your video ranks.

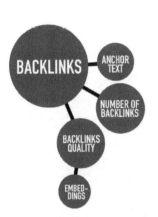

Backlinks – These are links from other sites that point toward your video or channel. Important elements include the anchor text (text of the link), the number of backlinks, and the quality of the backlinks (Trust Flow, Domain Authority), and number of video embeds.

Sharing –

Social signals are very important and gives an indication how interesting and engaging a video is. This includes shares on various social media platforms, especially Google+, Facebook, Blogger, LinkedIn and Twitter. Likes, favorites, pluses and retweets are all counted toward this factor.

102

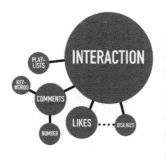

Interaction – YouTube wants its users to stay on its platform and engage with the content and community. Therefore, interaction plays a huge part in gauging how relevant a video is. Elements like how many playlists a video is added to, the number of comments on the video, if any relevant keywords are in the comments, and the number of likes and dislikes.

On-Page Video SEO

On-page SEO refers to every element you need to optimize that has to do with the video and the video page itself.

1) Video Filename

Before you upload your video you YouTube, you want to make sure the video filename has your main keyword in it. Do this with the video thumbnail as well. If possible, I also add the main keyword in the meta tags of the file. Depending on your operating system, you can do this by editing the file properties.

2) Video Title

The video title is the most important on-page SEO element of your video. You'll need to include the main keyword in here, as close as you can to the front. Then I recommend including a secondary YouTube keyword as well, separated by a pipe | symbol or hyphen.

For example, if your keyword is "how to make money on YouTube" and your secondary keyword is "how I make money on YouTube fast", then it would look like:

How To Make Money On YouTube – How I Make Money On YouTube Fast!

 Tip: *In addition to adding your keyword, it helps to craft an atten-tion-grabbing headline around it for maximum attention-grabbing potential.*

For example, I could transform the above into:

How To Make Money On YouTube – Watch How I Make Money on YouTube Fast in 24 Hours | With PROOF!

Now it reads more powerful and makes searchers want to click on the headline.

Alternatively, if you just want to go for a viral headline, go to BuzzSumo.com and enter your keyword. Look at the top trending article headlines for this topic and model one of them. If possible, try to include your keyword in the headline you write, otherwise you wouldn't be optimizing your video for ranking.

3) Video Tags

The video tags are a very important element that helps YouTube and Google understand what your video is about. This is how to create your tags:

Let's say the keyword is again, "how to make money on YouTube". I would create my tags like this:

How to make money on YouTube, how to make money, make money on YouTube, how to, make money, YouTube

In other words, I would include my main keyword, then chunk it down smaller and smaller.

Next, I would go on YouTube and search my main keyword. I would then click on the first ranked video and grab the tags in that video.

Super Tip: *Now, here's a ninja secret not many people know – normally, YouTube hides tags from the public, BUT if you're using Google Chrome Browser, or a browser that allows you to view the html, you can right click on the page and then select "view source". Then type ctrl+f (PC) or cmd+f (Mac), and type in "tags". There should be a list of tags that you can copy and paste at the end of your own list.*

Why are we doing this? Because for this keyword, YouTube has determined it is the most relevant, so by mirroring the tags, YouTube will see your video as closely related and will rank it higher in the search results.

4)   Video Description

The description is also a very important element that cannot be underestimated. The first three lines are the most important for two reasons: firstly, because it's the only part that's visible by default, until you click on the link to expand it. Secondly, because YouTube values the first lines the most in terms of looking for relevant keywords and understanding the meaning.

Tip: *What you need to do is put your main keyword in the first line, as close as you can to the front. If possible, copy and paste your title in the first line instead of including something else. The first three lines is also where you would put your main call to action link that you want people to visit.*

For the rest of the description, you'll need at least 300 words of content relating to the video keyword. Ideally, it would be 800-1,000 words so YouTube has more context to work with, but 300 is fine. You can either write the content, or paste the transcript in there.

Important: *Make sure the main keyword is in there at least once somewhere in the middle, and at least once near the end. Sprinkle some related keywords and some of the tags in there as well, but do it naturally, you don't want to "keyword stuff", which could have negative consequences.*

Add a few links into your description back to YouTube to give yourself some backlinks. Include a link back to the same video, and a link to your channel, and also a link to a video that is ranking in the top 3 positions for your keyword.

You should also link out to an authority blog post about that topic that gives YouTube and Google some more context to work with to understand your video better.

Closed Captions

By default, YouTube uses machine transcription to turn any speech into text for the closed captions or subtitles. Naturally, it's not perfect and can make errors, so it's best to edit and fix them.

Alternatively, you can get your video professionally transcribed and then upload the new subtitles, and set them as default.

Transcribe Your Video

The slow and painful (but free) way to transcribe your audio would be to do it yourself, however it's not fun, and can take up a lot of time you could use to focus on more content instead.

 Tools & Resources: *I would recommend using a really good service called Rev.com where you can get videos transcribed and turned into closed captions for only $1 a minute.*

If you want to reach a larger audience, you can also get your closed captions translated into another language, but it's not necessary.

5)   Publish Your Video

Once you have your video details entered and your thumbnail uploaded, you're ready to publish it. As soon as you do, start sharing it on social media, and start building backlinks and embeds. This is when off-page video SEO comes into play. Don't worry, we'll talk more about this in the Promote Your Videos chapter.

Off-Page Video SEO

Off-page video SEO has to do with every element that needs to be optimized off the main video or channel page, like links pointing to the video or channel from other YouTube videos/channels, or external websites or social media profiles. Social mentions and activity also play a large role in off-page SEO.

Backlinks

What is a backlink? A backlink is simply a link that is pointing from another website, video, or social media profile to your page.

Why are backlinks important?

Think of each backlink as a vote, and each vote has different levels of authority. Just in the same way that a 100 testimonials from people you don't know will have less influence than 10 testimonials from celebrities or industry leaders.

The more votes a website has, and the higher the authority, the more the website is likely to be trustworthy and relevant in the eyes of Google or

YouTube. This means it's more likely to rank higher for any given relevant search term.

Why do I need high quality backlinks?

When we talk about "high quality" backlinks, I'm mainly referring to the domain authority (DA) and page authority (PA) score. The higher the domain or page authority, the more ranking "power" it has.

Tools & Resources: *Moz.com "Open Site Explorer" tool allows you to check pages' Domain Authority and Page Authority.*

What's also really important is relevant backlinks. Let's say your video is about "how to train your parrot to talk", then you'll want backlinks from websites, blogs, forums, and other videos and channels that closely relate to the topic. Otherwise, the links would count much less or even change the context of your video topic.

How do you get high quality backlinks?

There are two ways you can do it: Do it yourself, or outsource them. Both have their pros and cons.

Building your own backlinks can be a lot of work and takes time, but you have more control over it and have full transparency of where you link from. It can also be less expensive if done through guest posts, on your own websites, or other free ways.

Outsourcing backlinks can be a tricky minefield if you don't know what to look for. The advantage is you save a lot of time.

There are a lot of sellers on the market where their backlinks just don't work or could even harm your video ranking performance. On the other hand, if you find the right providers, you'll be able to scale up your efforts without extra time.

A good place to look for backlinks is Fiverr.com or SEOClerks.com. The best way to determine whether the backlinks are good are to purchase from top rated sellers with a lot of 5 star reviews, and finally, just test and track your results using a keyword rank tracking software. If they are quality back-links, your video should start seeing some ranking improvements.

 Tools & Resources:

SEO Clerks - vidtr.in/seoclerks

This is an amazing platform for all services relating to SEO, from buy-ing backlinks, social signals, and much more. Make sure you buy from a trusted provider by looking at the ratings first.

You may have to test many providers before you find ones that work best. Always make sure they do "whitehat" and Google-friendly practices so your video or channel won't get penalized for bad links.

Video Embedding

Embedding your video on external websites is also a signal that YouTube looks for when ranking your video. You should embed your videos on your website and blogs to get more backlinks and external views on your videos, all which contribute to helping your ranking.

Again, make sure you embed on relevant pages and websites that relate to your video topic.

Video Playlists

Add your video into a relevant playlist. Playlists are searchable in YouTube, so create a playlist with relevant videos, including your own, and use a similar keyword. This will definitely boost your ranking, even if just a little bit.

Social Signals

Social media has become increasingly important, not only as a way to connect & engage with your audience, but also for search engines to determine how popular and relevant a website or video is by looking at social signals.

What are social signals?

Social signals are any activity on social media platforms that mention or link to your video or channel page. They include engagement signals like shares, likes, favorites, and comments.

Build backlinks to your video by posting it on social media. You will also be able to reach a lot more people and get people to watch and interact with your video. If they share it, you'll get the added benefit of reaching an even larger network you wouldn't have been able to otherwise.

 Action Step: *Post your video on as many as your social media platform as possible, like Google+, Facebook, Twitter, LinkedIn, Pinterest, Instagram and others.*

Why are social signals important?

YouTube or Google are smart, but they can't evaluate whether the video content itself is actually any good. They rely on social signals and the reactions of others to see how interesting a video is.

The idea is, the more shares, likes, and comments a post has, the more engaging and interesting a video is assumed to be.

How to get more social engagements on your videos

If you want to get more social interaction and engagements on your video posts in social media, try these ideas:

- Have an eye-catching thumbnail that stops the viewer from scrolling down the feed
- Add a benefit-based, curiosity-instilling headline
- Let them know what's in it for them, what will they learn?
- Tell them exactly what to do: LIKE, COMMENT, and SHARE!
- Post at times when most of your audience is active on the platform (use TubeBuddy.com)

Tools & Resources:

TubeBuddy - vidtr.in/tbud

This Google Chrome plugin is also a must-have for any YouTuber. It has way more features than VidIQ and adds advanced functionality to YouTube such as bulk processing, video SEO, promotion, and data research. There are too many features to mention here, but in short, it makes things so much easier and faster to use. Definitely download and install it.

CHAPTER **11**

Monetize Your Videos

T o make money via YouTube, it's vital that you know your business strategy.

When you have a clearly defined business model for your YouTube channel, then all your video content and call to actions can be aligned for that one common goal.

The free traffic you generate on YouTube can be very valuable, but you'd be surprised how few YouTubers know how to monetize that traffic in the best ways possible.

You need to ask yourself: **What will you use this traffic for? What's your end outcome?**

Is it to build an email list? Is it to build up your social media following on another platform? Is it to get more interaction and eyeballs on your blog? Is it to generate more sales? Is it to raise money for a charity? Or is it to fill an event?

Idea List: *Maybe you don't know how you can use the traffic. If you're unsure, here are some ideas:*

- Create funny/viral videos that get 6 or 7-figure views and then monetize your channel with YouTube AdSense.
- Have links to various landing pages where visitors can enter their email in exchange for a relevant and valuable free download, to build your email list. Then build a relationship with them by giving value and offering occasional products.
- Review digital software products and link them to the product with your affiliate link.
- Review Amazon products and link them to the product with your affiliate link.
- Drive traffic to your ecommerce store to get more product sales.
- Build up your Twitter/Facebook/Instagram/LinkedIn following, and then market products or services through those channels.
- Get them to join a private VIP Facebook group where you can interact with them regularly, add value, and eventually get them onto your email list and marketing funnel.
- A/B split test sales copy or optin pages so you can see which version works best before you actually pay for traffic.
- Sign them up to a $5-10/mo membership site delivering them 10x more value than they are paying for, then upsell them to a $97/mo program with even more value, to create some decent residual income.
- Get them to download your iOS/Android app if you have one.
- Link them to a CPA (cost per action) offer and get paid every time someone fills out a form, downloads/installs an app, or trials a product for free.

Tools & Resources:

MaxBounty - vidtr.in/mbty

A pretty large selection of CPA offers you can sign up to here.

Tools & Resources:

PeerFly - vidtr.in/pfly

This network also has a good reputation and range of CPA offers to choose from.

Tools & Resources:

FlexOffers - vidtr.in/flxo

Another good CPA network you can explore as well. Check it out.

- Generate leads for businesses in your niche by driving your YouTube traffic to a landing page and give something away for free in exchange for their email, then sell the leads at a premium price.
- "Rent" out the first line of your YouTube video description for top performing or ranking videos, so clients can put a relevant link there for a flat monthly fee. What you need to do is have the client pay you a flat monthly fee and then in exchange put the link they give you in the first line of your description.
- Sell clicks to clients' websites from specific videos, so you could charge $0.25-$1.00+ per click, depending on how targeted the traffic is. What you need to do is shorten their link in bitly.com or goo.gl and then at the end of the month, look at the statistics

on how many clicks it got and charge them based on how many there were.

Tools & Resources:

Bitly.com or Goo.gl - Use these websites to shorten your URLs and track how many clicks you get to your link. They both have good analytics dashboards and a QR code generator.

- Create 6-12 free tutorial videos or video lessons, then create 36-120 additional videos that they can purchase as a product on your website.
- Get them to register for regular webinars where you add value and at the end present them with a $500-$2,000 irresistible offer.
- Get them to register for live events or seminars in a specific location.
- Interview experts in your niche and give 25% of them away for free on the channel, then link to your site and offer some more interviews in exchange for their email, then upsell them the rest + monthly ones for a membership fee.
- Sell advertising spots on your high viewed videos to brands or similar businesses in your niche. Calculate the cost by the second.

Now, obviously this list is just a fraction of the thousands of ways you could use your YouTube traffic, but hopefully these will have given you some ideas and got your imagination flowing to come up with your own.

Action Step: *Choose ONE to begin with, then once you've mastered it successfully and gotten good results, you can start adding a second one, and so on. If you do too many at once, it splits your focus and makes it harder to track and see what's working and what's not.*

CHAPTER 12

Promote Your Videos

G reat, so you've published your video and started sharing it on your various social media platforms and linking it from your related websites. It's now time to promote your videos so you can get it seen by as many people in your target audience as possible. In this chapter, you'll learn both paid and free ways to promote your videos.

What if you don't have a large enough following and aren't getting the initial views, likes, comments, and shares you want? Then there's always the option to boost your video.

Boosting Your Video and Social Signals

There are two ways you can get an initial burst of video views and social signals.

1)   The first way is to do it manually, but that usually requires you to have an initial following or audience of some sort to promote your video to.

2)   The second way, which is perfect for when you're just starting out, is to purchase video views, likes and social shares.

I've seen my videos go from no ranking to first page position, just with a few thousand high retention views from a good source. It's very powerful!

You may or may not feel that buying views/likes/shares is right for you. It definitely doesn't fall into the "whitehat" category of techniques, but it works.

A disclaimer: Although the services I've personally have used have worked really well in ranking my videos, and I never ever had any problems with them, some vendors may not be so good and could get your channel or account shut down or penalized. If you do choose to go this route, do so at your own risk.

That being said, if you do choose to boost your videos with views and likes, I would make sure the services have a good track record, rating, and lots of good reviews. To do this, read the reviews and make sure there are at least 100+ 5 star reviews and the ratio of 5 star to lower ratings is really high.

Make sure the views are "high retention", meaning the 'viewers' watch over 50-70% of the video. YouTube loves these types of views and will rank your video much much higher. Most of the legitimate YouTube boosting services will tell you if their views are high retention or not. You can also just ask the seller if they are.

You can also get video likes, dislikes, and social media shares on Google+, Facebook, Twitter, etc. Depending on the seller, you can expect to pay between $5-20 per 1,000 high retention views, 100 likes, or 50 shares.

 Important: *The key is to make sure it looks as natural as possible, as if it had naturally occurred over time.*

Super Tip: *Stick to a ratio of 1,000:100:10, meaning, for every 1,000 views, there should be roughly 100 likes and 10 dislikes.*

Getting comments is also very important if you want YouTube to start recommending your video in the related videos sidebar or at the end of related videos.

Tip: *If you can, get your friends to leave a legit comment on your video, preferably mentioning the keyword or a tag phrase. What I mean, is instead of just commenting one word like "cool" or "nice", have something with more substance, like "Hey, I really enjoyed your video, especially when you were talking about how to rank your videos in 3 minutes on Google. I'll give this a try!".*

---

10 Free Ways to Get More Video Views

If your video genuinely adds value, then people are grateful if you share it with them. In many cases, videos are perceived less as promotions than if you were to share a link to your blog post or website.

Tip: *If you're not sure how to get more views of your videos for free, without buying them, then try these free strategies.*

Idea List: Here are a few free ways to get more video views:

- Share your video on all your social media pro-files.
- If you already have an email list, send out an email linking to your video.
- Post your video to all your relevant websites and blogs.
- Share your video in relevant Facebook groups.
- Share your video on niche forums, have it either as part of a response to a question someone is having, or include it in your post signature.
- Answer questions on Quora.com.

- Answer questions on Twitter using advanced search.
- Cross-promote your video with someone else - you promote their video in exchange for them promoting yours on their social media accounts.
- Do a guest blog post on a relevant niche blog with decent traffic. You can reach out to bloggers via their contact page, or go on Fiverr.com and purchase a "guest post" gig. Offer to write a high quality 500-800 word article and then embed your video in there to compliment the content.
- Collaborate with other YouTubers by reaching out to them via their email or via YouTube messages and cross-promote your videos in the end screens or annotations.

CHAPTER 13

Track Your Video Results

I f you can't measure something, you can't improve it. Peter Drucker, a management consultant, educator, and author, is often quoted as saying that "you can't manage what you can't measure".

The same is true with your YouTube videos. You need to quantify your current performance so you can track your progress and improvement.

YouTube Keyword Rank Tracking

There's no point doing all this work to rank your videos if you aren't able to see results and improve them over time. That's why you'll need to track your video ranking over time.

There are many tools you can use to track your keyword positions of your videos both in YouTube and Google.

I personally use SerpBook, but you can also use Advanced Web Ranking (AWR), which gives you more keywords per month. If you want more frequent keyword rank updates during the day, go with Serpbook, however, you'll get less number of keywords per month. If you want to track a larger number of keywords, then AWR is better and more cost effective.

Tools & Resources:

SerpBook - vidtr.in/serpbook

This tool allows you track your keyword positions for your videos in both YouTube, Google and other major search engines in different countries, desktop and mobile. The cool thing about this tool is you can have it check multiple times per day and on-demand. I highly recommend it.

 Tools & Resources:

Advanced Web Ranking - vidtr.in/awr

If you're looking for more keyword credits, then AWR is a better choice. It's also a decent keyword tracker for all the major search engines including YouTube. It also has international ability and is able to track on desktop and mobile platforms.

 Action Step: *Add your YouTube video URL and the keyword you want to track the ranking for, and then select how often you want the tool to check and track the ranking. Set to once per day by default.*

 Tip: *Make sure you use the full YouTube URL (https://www.youtube.com/watch?v=xxxxxxxxxx) and not the shortened version (https://youtu.be/xxxxxxxxxx).*

Sometimes, you may experience your video dropping out of the search results or moving positions. If so, YouTube is still trying to figure out how relevant your video is for that keyword and it should eventually stabilize.

Tip: *When you track your video ranking for Google, make sure to select "exact URL", otherwise the tool may just pick up any video that is ranked.*

You'll want to tweak the on-page elements over time to see whether you can improve the video ranking and minimize this movement. You can do this by experimenting with adding in more secondary keyword phrases, expanding the description, changing the tags slightly, fixing the closed captions, or adjusting the title.

Link Tracking

Tracking your link metrics is very important so you can get a click-through-rate (CTR) metric you can track and improve.

 Tools & Resources: *I recommend using a link shortener service such as goo.gl or bitly.com where you can both shorten a long url and see how many clicks you've gotten over time and where they have come from.*

The benefit of doing this is so that a really long URL looks more attractive and it doesn't take up so much space. It also hides the affiliate details of the link.

This is an example of one of my YouTube videos using a goo.gl link:

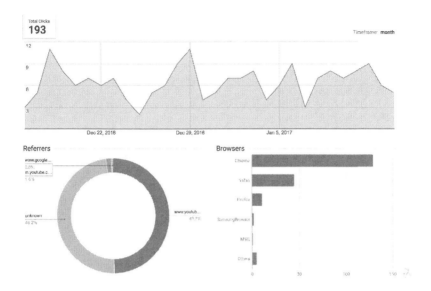

If you prefer, you can also create your own link shortener with your own domain and then use a Wordpress plugin called Pretty Link.

That way, you can customize the URL a bit more and also do split tests between multiple URLs with the Pro version.

 Tools & Resources:

Pretty Link - vidtr.in/prettylink

This Wordpress plugin allows you to create custom URLs and redirects with your own domain. You can also split test links and cloak links so others can't see the hidden URL. It's really useful!

Google Analytics

 Tip: *For recording traffic statistics on your website or landing page, I highly recommend using Google Analytics so you can see detailed statistics on how much traffic you get on your website, how long visitors stay, and where they go on your site.*

Simply sign up for free with your Google account and once you enter your website information, you'll be given an ID or code, which you put in the <head> section of your website. If you don't know how, you can get a webmaster to do this for you, or get a plugin if you use Wordpress where you just add the analytics ID.

You'll then be able to track the traffic, journeys, and visits to your site for more detailed analytics.

PART 3:
YOUTUBE EXPERTS

CHAPTER 14

Troy Adashun:
How to Get 120+ Videos on the First Page of YouTube

Chapter Overview

In this interview, you'll learn how Troy got over 160,000 Youtube subscribers, 20 million views, and rank over 120 videos on the first page of YouTube with zero dollars spent on YouTube advertising.

Connect With Troy

Websites: www.scienceofabs.com & www.superhumanyou.net

YouTube: @WeightGainNetwork - "Weight Gain Network" - For all the naturally skinny guys out there trying to gain weight

YouTube: @SpitThatReal - "Super Human You" - A mix of different topics including fitness, athlete training, success, and personal development

Twitter: @TroyAdashun
Facebook: @da.troy.3

T roy Adashun went to a prestigious sports academy from high school called IMG Academy in Bradenton, Florida. It was his dream ever since he was a little kid to play professional basketball, so he went to a really good training academy geared toward young athletes and became part of the basketball academy there.

Unfortunately, he never made the MBA, never grew past 6'1", and had his career cut short in college.

Things took a turn one day when he was in the weight room and saw all these guys preparing for the NFL drive. They would come to his school and train before the NFL combine.

These athletes were 230 lbs of pure muscle and were able to lift 300-400 lbs. Being young and impressionable, Troy looked up to them and wondered whether he could ever do the same.

This inspired him to start getting into fitness and lifting weights, and he realized quite quickly it not only transformed his life physically, but mentally as well when he started to see some progress and success in it.

It was a natural transition for him to go from playing basketball as a sport to dedicating his life to fitness.

Troy Discovers the World of Internet Marketing

Troy started to do personal training and soon got into fitness modeling, but he quickly found out that it was fiercely competitive and didn't have that much money in it unless you're at the top of the pack.

With not many options left, Troy discovered and started getting involved in the marketing world. The classic book most budding marketers read is the **Four Hour Work Week** by **Timothy Ferriss** (vidtr.in/4hww). He also read

Millionaire Fastlane by **MJ DeMarco** (vidtr.in/mfastln) and soon after met this guy who was really into YouTube at the time.

The YouTube guy's channel he was doing at the time, which 3-4 years ago wasn't that popular yet, but exploded just a few years later. Troy thought it was really cool and wanted to start making videos himself, so this encounter sparked his initial interest in it.

Soon after, he partnered with a guy who actually had some marketing experience. Troy thought at the time that he knew what he was doing, but in fact, he was actually quite green with online marketing.

This marketing guy worked for a digital publishing company and Troy has been working with him on the **Weight Gain Network** (@WeightGainNetwork) YouTube channel ever since.

He learned a lot from him about online marketing such as how to properly do call to actions for each video to increase engagement and how to align the marketing messages to actually monetize the videos.

Most people need to be told exactly what to do. For example: "Click on the link below", "Tap on the thumbs up", "Tell me what you think in the comments".

 Tip: *Every video should have a call to action if you want to lead them to the next step in the marketing process so you can get more subscribers, leads and sales.*

Troy's Biggest Challenge – the Keyword Conundrum

One of the biggest challenges for Troy was doing the keyword research for the videos to try and rank them high in the search results.

Trying first with **Google Keyword Planner** (vidtr.in/kwplanner) to find search volume for different keywords didn't quite translate well to YouTube's actual keyword volume. In fact, he found out even though these two search engines were quite similar, they were also different in many ways as well.

Finally, he cracked the code – he decided to mostly ignore the Google Keyword Planner and just focus all his research on the YouTube platform to rank his videos on there.

The solution was to **just type things into the YouTube search bar** and see what suggestions came up, what's really popular, then create a video around that topic and put his own creative angle on it.

Super Tip: *When you start typing in something into the YouTube search bar, you'll see YouTube suggest phrases.*

The first and the last words usually catch your eye the most, so using one of these is a good place to start when choosing your keywords.

Troy found noticeable results in his ranking when using keywords with this method.

how to gain mu
how to gain muscle
how to gain muscle fast
how to gain muscle mass
how to gain muscle mass for skinny guys
how to gain muscle and lose body fat
how to gain muscle without weights
how to gain muscle at home
how to gain muscle for women
how to gain muscle fast for skinny guys
how to gain muscle fast for teenagers

How to Easily Get a Million Video Views

Troy found out that the combination of a really good thumbnail and a really good title is the key to getting a lot of views and rank high on YouTube.

The title has to be more than just the keyword and must add some element of interest, curiosity, or "click bait" as they call it. It should be a nicely crafted title similar to what an effective blog post would have - something that grabs their attention, and that gets them to click and watch it.

For example, Troy has one video about "How To Get Big Arms", which is a pretty popular search in the fitness and bodybuilding niche, so to get it more "clickbait-esque" is he crafted the title "The 5 Commandments of Getting Big Arms". This added authority and made it a little bit more fun as well.

He put a lot of effort into **adding text onto his thumbnails** to get attention and stand out from the competition. He did this by working with a graphic designer who created his custom thumbnails, which actually turned out to be really cheap.

 Super Tip: *You can hire talented designers to design a high quality YouTube thumbnail as little as $5-10. You can go to vidtr.in/fiverr and search for "YouTube Thumbnail" and sort by highest rated gigs first for the best quality ones.*

How to Model the Top YouTubers' Success

The number one thing to keep in mind if you want to get successful on YouTube is to put a lot of thought into the call to action in your videos.

The best way to learn is to pay close attention to the marketing YouTubers – like "Tai Lopez" (@tailopezofficial) and the other big YouTubers of the world (see https://socialblade.com/youtube/top/100) and model how they structure their videos and call to action.

Then, actually click on their links and go through their funnels while taking a look at the landing pages that you go on. Notice how natural the transition is from the call to action that you came from in the video to the landing page. **The key is being aware of all these details.**

When he's setting up and monetizing a new YouTube channel and building out all these landing pages, Troy immerses himself in studying what all these successful marketers and YouTubers are doing.

 Tools & Resources:

Thrive Content Builder and Landing Pages - vidtr.in/tcb

If you have your own Wordpress website or are planning to build one (not wordpress.com, but the .org version), then I highly recommend using this Wordpress plugin. I use it on all my websites where I need an easy drag-n-drop editor and landing page functionality with a lot of ready-to-edit templates. Really powerful and amazing value for what you pay. It also saves a lot of time and frustration!

 Tools & Resources:

ClickFunnels - vidtr.in/cf

Definitely one of the most complete Internet marketing, landing page and funnel software I've ever seen. It uses the latest technology and has a ton of powerful features to easily and quickly creates high converting marketing funnels and landing pages. I couldn't recommend it enough! You can try it for free for 30 days.

He pays particular close attention to not only the title, but also the "vibe" or look and feel of the design of the page. There are so many different elements and possible variations that go into it.

For example, does it go straight to a headline where you need to enter an email, or does it land on a sales video with a call to action button?

The type of landing page you create really depends on your preference. Troy loves being in front of the camera, as he was actually training to be an actor about 6 years ago, so it was quite natural for him to do that. On his landing pages he usually puts a video.

Tools & Resources:

LeadPages - vidtr.in/lpgs

If you want a lighter weight landing page software without having to build your own website, then this will do the job for collecting leads and building your list. I definitely would check it out.

But if you're not comfortable with that, then just study the people who have really good headlines, and really good landing pages with text copy. In other words, you'll need to become a really good copywriter or hire a professional copywriter to craft your landing page or sales page.

Super Tip: *Hiring a good copywriter can be expensive, but well worth it. When you do find someone you think is good, ask them what kind of results they've gotten for their clients. What was the conversion rate? How many sales did they get? It can be a challenge to find someone good, but it will pay off in the end if you have a quality product or service you're promoting.*

How to Get Views Really Quickly on a Brand New Channel

The first thing Troy would do on a brand new channel is he would start grabbing the "low hanging fruit", which means **collaborating with other YouTubers who have between 2,000 and 10,000 subscribers.**

The influencers at this level are still accessible but at the same time produce high quality content, which if you aligned with, would definitely benefit your channel really quickly!

Tip: *Go on YouTube and make a list of all the YouTube channels in your niche that have between 2k-10k subscribers. Then, contact each one by going to the "about" tab on their channel and click "Send message" and ask them if they would be open to collaborating. Remember, approach it with the intent of creating a long-term mutually beneficial relationship.*

Tip: *It goes without saying that at the end of the day, just make sure to create really awesome content and be a little bit different – just be yourself and authentic!*

The people that Troy's seen who have really started to "blow up" on YouTube are those who are different, but at the same time are still themselves - with a unique personality, flaws, and honesty.

The best way to describe these people would be "polarizing". Be polarizing if you want to attract a huge following of loyal fans.

Polarizing means that you have strong opinions about certain things and you don't care if you piss people off.

As a result, you will create two distinct groups of people: "haters" who hate you and "raving fans" who absolutely love you.

You need to be confident to be yourself and must be OK with people seeing your imperfections, weaknesses and personal challenges.

Troy said he made this mistake too back when he was creating a lot of content 3-4 years ago on his channel The Weight Gain Network (now over 155,000+ subscribers). He wasn't fully confident and even though it got him excited to be in front of the camera, he felt he wasn't being his true self because of fear of taking chances.

Tip: *The key is once you stop caring what other people think and that is completely eliminated from the back of your mind, that's when you can really make a lasting impact on YouTube.*

Get Clear on Your Business Model So You Can Make Money ASAP

Define exactly what your business model is. For example, Troy loves creating information products and believes he brings a lot on the table with unique solutions to common fitness and bodybuilding problems that he went through himself, which he had to overcome.

Action Step: *Learn all the ways to make money on YouTube and know your end goal – maybe you want to become a live speaker, a 1-on-1 coach, or whatever your area of expertise is, so make sure you study the different ways you can monetize that.*

YouTube Business Model Ideas

- Review affiliate products, either physical or virtual
- Build an email list and offer progressive higher value products to your subscribers as they go through your marketing funnel
- Create an ecommerce store and use YouTube to drive traffic to it
- Build a massive subscriber base on YouTube and sell advertising slots in your videos
- Fill regular webinar presentations & convert attendees on a high-end offer
- Rent the first few lines of the video description space to someone for a video with high daily views for a monthly fee

How to Go from $0 to Quitting Your Job FAST!

If you're already an expert at something, without a doubt, the best strategy to make really fast money, like from going from $0 to quitting your job, would be to **offer coaching or consulting services by advertising through YouTube.**

You would use the traffic you generate from your YouTube videos to build up an **email list.** Then you would follow up with them by sending them tips and useful information via emails. Once the trust is established, show them how you can help them by offering your coaching or consulting services.

 Tools & Resources:

Ontraport - vidtr.in/ontra

Probably one of the best higher-end email marketing software with advanced automation features and other powerful features. Check it out - it's best for if you have a larger list or need the more detailed features it provides.

 Tools & Resources:

Aweber - vidtr.in/aweb

I've used this email autoresponder service for many years; it's really good and has everything you expect to need in an email autoresponder. It also integrates with most services out there, so is very flexible.

Tools & Resources:

Mailchimp - vidtr.in/mchp

If you want to start out with something free, then I recommend Mail-Chimp. The free version allows you to build an email list up to 2,000 subscribers and send broadcast messages out. If you want automation, then you'll need to upgrade.

For him in the fitness niche, he still does online coaching and he finds that there are still lots of people who reach out to him without even knowing he offers this and if he would be willing to set up a custom meal or workout plan.

This can apply to pretty much any niche. It's the easiest because there's no overhead; all that's needed is just sharing your advice and knowledge by coaching them one on one over the phone or video chat online.

Once you have them on your email list (via landing page), have made the sale (through PayPal), and booked a coaching session (Calendly.com), then you can do the actual session using Skype or Google Hangouts.

Tools & Resources:

Calendly.com - This is a great platform to book in meetings or appointments with others. It's free and integrates with your calendar. You can also block out times when you're not available.

Alternatively, if that's too complicated for you, then you can just have them contact you via email, ask them to send you the agreed payment amount for your session, and then hop on Skype on the date you book.

Coaching is also a perfect way to start if you're not really good with technology and don't know about autoresponders, email marketing, or websites.

It could be too overwhelming for you at the beginning, so just focus on bringing in the money and offering a service.

A lot of people who have experience in a subject area have this false belief that they aren't **an "expert" or they aren't ready to coach yet. What they don't realize is that an expert is simply someone who knows more than the audience they are sharing the information with**. There's always something you will know that somebody else doesn't know. Give yourself some credit; start sharing your knowledge and charge for it!

Vlogging on YouTube is the Future

One really big thing he sees changing that has forced him to step up his game and re-evaluate his content is that he's seeing the best YouTubers doing an awesome job at letting you in on their personal life. This trend of "Vlogging" is becoming really popular, no matter what you do.

For example, Tai Lopez (@tailopezofficial) is a famous Internet entrepreneur who is known on YouTube for his "Here In My Garage" Lamborghini video.

He has a lot of great value to share on business, books, learning, and living the "Good Life" as he calls it, which is the typical dream of having a lot of money, nice cars, great relationships, and the house of your dreams.

The average person who watches him knows more about his life than they do some of their friends. Crazy right? It's because he does a really good job of letting you in on his personal life - his friends, inside jokes and stories.

 Important: *Be really personal and teach something, while also being entertaining (also known as "edutainment").*

137

When you watch the good YouTubers stand in front of you, sharing with you the steps to learning something, it actually engages you in a different way because people's attention span is so short right now.

Troy calls this type of content sharing a **"misdirect"**. For example, let's say he's doing a video on "5 Fatloss Tips". Instead of talking in front of a camera saying this is what you got to do: step 1, step 2, step 3… it's a much better video and a lot more engaging if, while he's playing tennis, he's talking about a couple different things, but also going through the steps.

Good YouTubers do a really good job of telling stories while going through their tips. It's something Troy's going to start to incorporate into his videos more often.

Interestingly, if you go on YouTube and look at the videos 3 or 4 years ago, absolutely nobody was doing that. They almost treated it like they were on a TV show and had a camera guy with a professional camera. You can't treat it like that anymore - you got to have fun, be casual, and not take it too seriously.

These days, if you take a look at a lot of the style of videos, people are just holding their phones and filming themselves. If you look at the majority of successful YouTubers, they have a lot of videos where they are in their car (or wherever they are) and they are using their phone for selfie-style videos. It's an interesting change that has happened in the last couple of years.

How to Increase Your YouTube Video Performance

The videos that Troy's seen that do the best in terms of ranking on Google and YouTube have **the most social interaction and best average watch time.** YouTube is a community and they want people to be interacting with their videos.

Important: *You can structure your video in the perfect way - the perfect title, the perfect keywords, the perfect everything - but if the first 1,000 people to land on your five minute video only watch it for a minute and seven seconds, the rest doesn't matter.*

The amazing thing about YouTube is that you can't really cheat the system. There's been some "blackhat" tactics exposed in the last 10 years by Google, but there's really no way to cheat the system on YouTube. Why?

Because even if you get your video on the first page of YouTube using shady tactics, at the end of the day the video is going to be up there and people are going to click on it. If they don't interact or watch it for more than a couple minutes, then it's going to shoot down the rankings really quickly.

Obviously, having everything optimized like your title, keywords, and description is still very important.

Tip: *Include at least **5-10 related keywords in your video description text** and also **add a few links to resources**. For example, add a link to an article on how to lose weight. The best way to do this is to find an article on an **authority website** (a website that is trustworthy and has a lot of high-quality backlinks to it).*

Super Tip: *Use Moz.com's Open Site Explorer tool to check the Domain Authority (DA) score (0=None, 100=Maximum) of the website. Here's the quick link to the tool: vidtr.in/ose*

For example, you could find an article about how to lose weight and put it in your description to add more value to your viewers and give some more context to YouTube of what the video is about.

Tip: *Another powerful tactic is to get a guest post on a blog or website with good domain authority with a lot of traffic, which is super powerful, especially to rank in Google.*

Also if you can get your video shared on Google+ pages a lot, that really helps to boost the rankings. If you have a lot of friends or people in your Google Plus network, then ask them to share it.

 Important: *Just make sure you share your video on every social media profile you have - Facebook, Twitter, Instagram, Snapchat, LinkedIn, Google+ and others.*

How to Get the Money to Naturally Flow to You

If you want to be full time on YouTube, just make sure you really love the creative and art side of it and treat it like your own mini TV channel.

Fall in love with the process of creating awesome videos that are really engaging, captivate people, and get people to interact, then the money is just naturally going to come your way.

At the end of the day, make sure it's something you really love, and when you do find that topic, then for 6-12 months straight, put out the best quality content and don't even worry or think about the money.

Make sure you niche your topic down too, which is becoming more important than ever right now. Even though there are so many amazing opportunities and ways to make money, YouTube is becoming a lot more competitive. The solution to this is to define your niche and exactly who your perfect future customer or target audience is.

Tools & Resources: *To find out what words and phrases your audience uses, go on Reddit.com (a social news aggregation, web content rating, and discussion website) and dive into some sub-Reddits (sub topics) to see what kind of questions people there have.*

This can be really powerful for coming up with content ideas and get inside the mind of your target market.

Additional Content

Watch the full exclusive YouTube VIP interview here:

http://vidtr.in/troy

CHAPTER 15

Tim Han:
How to Get over 50,000
Subscribers in 3 Days

Chapter Overview

In this interview, you'll learn how Tim got over 50,000 YouTube subscribers in 3 days and sold out his coaching practice for 5 months, literally overnight!

Connect With Tim

Website: www.successinsider.tv

YouTube Channel: "Success Insider"

Twitter: @SuccessInsideTV
Facebook Group: @SuccessInsider

I was following Tim Han on Facebook through a mutual friend and learned that he became really successful through YouTube, so I decided to reach out to him and find out more.

I found out soon after that Tim had amassed over 50,000 YouTube subscribers in only 3 days and sold out his coaching practice for five whole months virtually overnight.

Tim Han is a celebrity YouTuber, performance coach, digital marketing expert and speaker, but it wasn't always so successful for him…

He was originally born in Seoul, South Korea and grew up with a single mum because his father left him at the age of two. They spent many years in Korea and then moved to the UK to start a new life in a very small town in England.

Things were tough – Tim was the only Asian guy in the area, and he had to deal with a lot of bullying at school, which was really hard on him as he grew up.

In high school, Tim made a big promise to himself to be willing to do whatever it takes to never ever face that pain again. He decided to hang around the "cool kids". So that's exactly what he did…

The problem was that all the cool kids at the time were hanging around in gangs, committing crimes, and dealing drugs. He had to make a choice – to take everything or nothing at all.

His friends were taking drugs, but then he decided that wasn't enough for him – he wanted to start growing drugs! So he started to grow drugs, but still, this wasn't even enough. So Tim started robbing other drug dealers.

Everything changed for Tim on New Year's Day. He had his head down the toilet bowl because he drank too much the night before. At that moment, he thought "Tim, just try to get some sleep".

He ran to his bedroom and grabbed his laptop. He remembers jumping on YouTube, thinking that if he types in something like "presentation", that will probably send him to sleep.

What happened next changed his life. He typed in "presentation" and saw this video pop up from a guy called "Steve Jobs' 2005 Stanford Commencement Address". He had no idea who this guy was at the time and thought it looked super boring. He clicked on it thinking he was going to watch it for 2 minutes, but then ended up watching the whole thing.

At that moment, Tim realized he screwed up – but he was going to change it!

From then on, he decided that he just had to do something with his life. He remembers being inspired by videos of guys who were driving fast cars and sharing their incredible lifestyles.

It was then that he really discovered a lot about the Internet marketing industry. There are so many products out there that claim this big stuff, like making millions, and money falling from the sky. The truth is, it doesn't happen.

He wasted a lot of money during that period, however, he did hit upon something that allowed him to come up with a formula for himself.

One day he was flicking through a newspaper and it said, "You can buy luck and you'll be luckier". At first glance he thought it was stupid, but he decided to try it anyways…

Tim started to sell "Luck" on eBay and it turned out it sold quite well.

As a 17-year old, he was like "Wow, this is incredible, I can sell this stupid stuff… imagine if I actually come up with something?!"

That was the beginning of Tim's online journey. He started to get into music because his friends said he was terrible at it, so he decided to prove them all wrong and create a YouTube channel (@DjTimoT2384), which went on to rack up over a million views overall.

The success of this channel allowed Tim to create a clubbing events business and got his name out there as a DJ.

Seven years later, he created a new channel called "Success Insider" (vidtr.in/successinsider), which had to do with personal development from his transformation journey.

How to Go from 10,000 To 1,000,000 Views in Less Than a Week

One of Tim's claim to fames was one of his videos that went viral from 10,000 views to over a million in just a few days. I asked him what the video was about and what he thought that got it to take off like that.

"It comes down to a lot of factors", he replied, and it's a question he's been asked a lot over the years.

On going viral, he saw a statistic saying that **you're more likely to die falling out of bed, than you are actually to go viral.** Crazy, right?!

But somehow, Tim managed to do it. One of the tools he used at the time was called Buzz Sumo (vidtr.in/buzz).

Buzz Sumo allows you to see blogs that have gone viral in the past. He had this idea of finding a blog post that's gone viral and then create it into a video.

He came across an article that had the headline of something like "Signs You'll Become Rich One Day". He knew at the time that using numbers in headlines is very good, but using odd numbers is even better.

According to marketing platform Outbrain.com, their "research has shown that headlines with odd-numbered lists have a 20% higher click-through rate than even-numbered ones". So he wrote "Three Signs You'll Become Rich One Day".

He published it and three months later, he got only 10,000 views and thought nothing's happening with it. Then, he had the intuition to start playing around with the thumbnail a bit. The current thumbnail of a picture of him, wasn't popping out at him.

He decided to use a photo of Jack Ma who is a Chinese business magnate and is the founder and executive chairman of Alibaba Group (Alibaba.com). He made the background black, so it really pops out on YouTube's white home page. Then he put big words like "Three Signs You'll Become Rich One Day".

A month later, his video had gone viral and he had made money from a combination of YouTube ads, affiliate products, and coaching.

A lot of the traffic he sends to Facebook, and as a result, built up a huge following community, which he believes is really important in regards to any brand you want to grow.

His biggest revenue stream comes from coaching clients. **Personal branding is key**, because the moment you do that, you can just raise your fees, because you're not being paid for what you do, but instead who you are.

Super Tip: *To get coaching clients, you need to first demonstrate you have value to offer. Start sharing your knowledge and experience in your field by creating YouTube videos with free tips and advice. If you don't have any experience in a field, then choose something that interests you, study it intensely for several months, and apply the information in your life by taking massive action. Then you'll start to have some experience and lessons to share.*

How to Avoid the Two Common Traps Most People Fall into

Trap #1: Putting yourself in a competitive and confined niche

Tim's biggest challenge in his journey where he sees a lot of people fail in regards to YouTube, especially for coaches, is that when you're coaching or doing some sort of consulting, you're **in a very confined niche.**

It's different than posting entertaining videos that gets shared like crazy. It's actually harder to make content about self-development skills because the traffic volume is not there.

Trap #2: Not being consistent with your YouTube video publishing

Tim says the biggest thing that he had trouble with when he started Success Insider is **consistency**. It's easy to get discouraged when you post a video and it doesn't get millions of views like you see on the comedy channels. You start to compare and then you ask the dangerous question "Should I really post that day?". Tim sticks to a strict schedule of when he posts.

He said that consistency can be broken with the pursuit of perfection. The real reason why people aren't consistent and the reason why he wasn't consistent is because he was pursuing perfection.

If Tim had to start from scratch again, the first thing he would do is **fix a specific time and date every single week that he's going to upload a video**. This is really important, because consistency is something that YouTube looks for.

 Action Step: *Create a content schedule for when you plan on posting your videos. Use Microsoft Excel or Google Sheets to keep track of the video content that will be posted next.*

He found that when he didn't maintain the weekly schedule, he noticed a massive drop on his YouTube channel, so he hasn't missed a week since.

When Tim was watching professionally-shot YouTube videos using advanced studio lights, fancy microphones and other expensive equipment, he asked himself if he really needed it.

He remembers buying the equipment but it turned out being a real fuss to set up and involved a lot more effort every time he had to record a video. As a result, he started judging his videos more for insignificant flaws.

This was the main reason why at times he procrastinated, but still managed to pump the video out. It's why people end of failing with this very common pattern.

Are You Fishing in a Small Pond?

Throughout his journey, he found an interesting thing. A lot of people who come to him are consultants, coaches, and business owners. If you're one of these people, you're fishing in a small pond. A lot of people out there don't realize that.

Let's say there's a coaching pond and all the other coaches are at this pond, fishing. The problem is, in this pond, there are only about five fish, but there are about one million coaches who have their rods out trying to catch a fish.

Tim's always been the one who finds this bigger pond, whereby there are thousands upon thousands of fish. But not very many coaches know about this big pond. In fact, in this big pond, you will find entertainment channels, not coaches.

What he does is go over to the big pond and start fishing there and starts getting this insane amount of traffic. That's how you really start pumping out successful YouTube channels.

That's the key – you shouldn't aim for viral, you should aim for sustainable growth! This comes only from these bigger ponds and discovering a strategy where you can find these big ponds in your niche.

 Super Tip: *To find these bigger ponds, all you have to do is ask yourself "What else is my target market interested in?" It's these secondary interests that are the ponds with much less competition than the primary interest that most marketers target.*

When he started Success Insider, which is mainly about productivity and performance, for the first six months he didn't post a single video to do with performance! It was all to do with dating. But, he still got clients to do with performance, because these people who were into productivity, were also interested in dating.

It's really about finding where your target market is. For example, if your target market is an entrepreneur, that's not their only passion. Maybe they really love football, right? That's the bigger pond! So you might create videos about football that would appeal to entrepreneurs. That way, you attract them to your channel through a "side door" (the bigger pond).

Action Step: *Brainstorm some of the possible "bigger ponds" that you can start to target for less competition. Think about your audience and some of the other interests they may have.*

What Tim Would Do If He Had to Start from Scratch Again

If Tim had to start over again, he would find a YouTube channel that is within his niche and model every single element they've used.

For example, if you're in the beauty niche, maybe you go to a beauty channel and you'll see the marketing funnel has a picture of their face and maybe a before and after makeup. You would copy it and put your face there instead.

Maybe they used a big, bold pink text in the middle, then maybe in the thumbnails, they've used some sort of eye-catching red borders that make it pop.

It's not a one-size-fits-all, you have to find out what works within your niche and just apply it on your own channel.

Once you've made it work, then you improve it. The problem is that people try to re-invent the wheel too much. Just realize what the platform is, who's dominating it, and copy them. Model success. It's as simple as that.

The Human-To-Human Connection Is Key

Vibrate from a level whereby you are genuinely trying to help others. Obviously the strategy really matters, but at the end of the day, remember, it's a human-to-human connection.

People can tell what your real agenda is when they're watching you. This is why videos by 2019, according to Cisco, are going to account for 80% of online consumption (vidtr.in/cisco). It's because videos are real – you can't be fake when somebody's just looking at you. You can hide behind a blog post, but not a video.

Always keep it real and be authentic. It may sound cliché, but very few people actually do what they know. Just be human, because this is another human you're interacting with.

Additional Content

Watch the full exclusive YouTube VIP interview here: http://vidtr.in/tim

CHAPTER 16

Michael Koehler: How to Make $50,000 from a Single YouTube Video

Chapter Overview

In this interview, you'll learn how Michael made $50,000 from a single YouTube video and how he built his social media agency from free traffic from YouTube.

Connect With Michael

Website: www.michaelkoehler.co.uk

YouTube Channel: "Michael Kohler"

Twitter: @xtremesocialug
Facebook: @michael.koehler.9699

I found Michael Koehler how most people do – by searching on YouTube. I was looking for "How to rank videos on YouTube" and clicked on his video, which was ranked 2nd out of 4,720,000 results. I was like, how did he do that?!

During his video, he mentioned he had a YouTube course, which I bought and learned many of the strategies I'm using today to also rank my videos on the first page of search results for virtually any keyword I want.

Michael's claim to fame is that he made over $50,000 from one single YouTube video using the ranking methods he learned over the years through lots of trial and error.

He went from being a broke college student to becoming a successful full-time online entrepreneur and social media expert. I reached out to him not long after I started applying his strategies and he agreed to share his story.

His First $10,000 Thanks to Small Services

It was about 3.5 years ago when Michael was still in college and didn't have much money. One day, he was typing into Google "how to make money online". He saw some stuff about filling out surveys and getting paid around $1 per survey. He tried that and it kind of worked.

Michael started to look a little bit further into how he could make more money online, as this survey site just wasn't cutting it.

He found this site called Fiverr.com where you can sell micro-services for $5 per service when you first start out. Later you can actually charge more as you acquire higher ratings and more sales.

Michael decided to put a service on there, and then pretty much forgot about it afterwards.

Two weeks later, his phone alerted him and he saw an email notification just arrived. "You've just made your first $5!" it said. It was actually $4 net for him, because 20% goes to Fiverr. He was impressed and thought, "Damn, this is really what I want to do!". If he could just scale it up, it would really pay off! He said it felt so great to make money with virtually no effort online, anywhere you are in the world.

He continued to create more services, generated more sales, and ended up raking in a total of $10,000 thanks to Fiverr.

During that time, he re-invested that money into his own website and developing his own services. He started to get clients that way and that's how he basically built up a successful social media agency.

Before creating his main personal YouTube channel (vidtr.in/mkc), he had many different channels covering a wide range of niches that were used to drive traffic to his websites. That's where he learned and cracked the code to ranking videos on YouTube.

Soon after, he thought it would be a smart thing to start his personal channel where he could position himself as an expert in the industry and teach people how to do things.

The $50,000 YouTube Video

When he first started on YouTube, Michael was all about quantity, so the goal was to upload as many videos as possible and try to rank them for lower competitive keywords instead of taking one or two high quality videos and rank them for very high competitive keywords to get a lot of traffic.

This was before he figured out how this whole ranking process works so he could rank videos for any keyword he wanted – both low and high competition.

He found some software (see Stoica Bogdan's interview) that helped him to generate relevant titles, descriptions, and tags.

Soon, one of the videos he had ranked for (which was about Twitter marketing) made over $50,000 in revenue from social media services and it was the first one where he unconsciously used these exact same ranking methods that he's teaching now. The success of this video was primarily because it was high quality, it was ranked very high, and it was also high converting.

Michael said that he didn't monetize his videos with Google AdSense, even though that's what most people thought. The thing is, if you're starting a YouTube channel and you're not really famous, the payout is not that great.

His strategy is to **create videos that always have a unique selling proposition that drives traffic to his website**. The key was linking the video to a landing page where he offered a social media management service. He gathered the leads through this landing page, built an email list, and followed up with them by offering them monthly recurring social media services.

How Michael Ranks Videos in the Top 5 Positions of Page 1

When you check out Michael's channel, you'll see a lot of tutorial videos. Most of his tutorial videos rank at least on the first page in one of the top five positions for the main keyword.

He has also noticed this phenomenon where keyword positions are "dancing", meaning they may drop in and out of certain positions before stabilizing. One day you may be in position 5. Next day you could be in position 40. Then you jump back on position 3 or something. This can happen when YouTube's algorithm is trying to determine how relevant your video is for that keyword.

It also depends a lot on your channel authority. The older your channel gets and the more subscribers you get, the more likely it is that you'll rank. Right now, when he uploads a new video, he ranks it in around one day. When he first started, it took him sometimes two months to rank a video in the first, second, or third position.

Top Ranking Tips for Newbies with Brand New Channels

1) First thing is to make sure you create a channel around a topic where there's an actual demand and people are searching for it so that if you rank for it, you will get traffic. If there's no demand, then you won't get many views, clicks or make much money. It's very simple.

2) Next, is you simply go on YouTube and type into the search bar what you think your target audience would type in. Then you see if it pops up in the suggested searches. Then you know that you can rank for this.

3) The third step is you need to know how to actually rank for it. For newer channels, it's a little bit harder when you only have a few subscribers because YouTube doesn't yet value your channel and content that much yet compared to your competitors with a larger following and more videos.

On YouTube, a lot of people really underestimate the title keywords, tags, and description, but most YouTube courses or videos are already teaching this.

He developed a method where he uses software that automatically generates the best and most relevant titles, descriptions, and tags (see Stoica Bogdan's interview).

156

This will make it way easier to rank, and then what you need to do is "boost" your video by promoting it through various social media accounts so it gets more views, likes, subscribers, and comments. Then it's pretty much ranked.

Do Something You Are Passionate About

Michael finds that a lot of people come to him who try to just create a channel to send traffic to their Amazon review page (to create affiliate sales), which they don't really care about.

He tells people they should really do something that they're actually passionate about when they start a YouTube channel. For example, he's really passionate about making these tutorials about social media. He now started this new format called "Ask Michael", where people can ask him questions and he responds with an answer in a video.

Passion is really important, because if you don't have the passion, you'll eventually lose interest in creating videos and you'll just stop. Then you'll most likely end up blaming it on something else like "This ranking method doesn't work" and you'll stop making videos. It's you, not the strategy, that's the factor.

It's not easy to start a company, but if you have passion, if you are addicted to what you do, then you can do it successfully, no matter what the challenge. That's the biggest piece of advice he would give people who are starting out.

 Super Tip: *If what you're passionate about is not an area with much demand on YouTube, then I suggest you tap into another passion you have. Discover more passions by becoming curious about different topics and learning more about them. Ask yourself "How can I use this information to improve my life?", "How can I use this information serve others?".*

Build Your Email List through YouTube Traffic

Out of all the ways to make money on YouTube, Michael suggests creating videos to send people to a landing page where you can gather their emails and find out what they are interested in, so you can follow up with them later.

 Tip: *This email list may take some time to build, so you might want to balance this strategy with a faster way to make money by offering affiliate products.*

It depends what kind of business you have. If you're selling services, then this is the way to go. It also creates long time value because you have leads where you can offer them products one, two, or even five years from now.

If you're just an affiliate and you sell someone else's product, you don't have an actual customer base. You have made a sale, but don't have a customer that you can build a relationship with over time.

Additional Content

 Watch the full exclusive YouTube VIP interview here:
http://vidtr.in/michael

CHAPTER 17

John Michael:
How to Earn $5,000 to $10,000
a month thanks to YouTube

Chapter Overview

In this interview, you'll learn how John went from overworked manager to earning $5,000 to $10,000 a month thanks to YouTube.

Connect With John

Website: www.johnmichaelmarketing.com

YouTube Channel: "John Michael"

Twitter: @johnminspires
Facebook: @johnmichaellifestyle

O n a 3-day Laptop Millionaire Retreat in Cyprus, I met John Michael.

John earns between $5,000 to $10,000 a month thanks to YouTube by getting free traffic from videos ranked on first page of Google and YouTube.

John's Story

Before his success, John had no idea what YouTube was. He was working as a food and beverage operations manager in a 5-star resort. He was exhausted, frustrated, and really looking for a way out.

At the time, he was working 10-12 hours a day, 6 to 7 days a week. He had no life.

One day, he happened to meet Mark at the resort playing tennis. Mark gave him his book "The Laptop Millionaire" to read (vidtr.in/laptopmillionaire). John was really excited and ended up reading it in only 2 days on top of his 12-hour per day job.

He went back home, started researching, and looking for how he can get this thing working. This went on for a while, but he wasn't really getting anywhere because he was working so long.

John Quit His Job & Made His First $250 on YouTube

One day, John decided to quit his job and start the journey. It was a very crazy and bold decision, with a lot of ups and downs – but mostly downs – to the point where he was almost completely broke because he had spent all his money on paid traffic that didn't end up converting into sales.

At this point, he had no other choice but to look into free ways of how to generate traffic. He wasn't willing to go back to a job and already had burned his boat.

That's when he turned toward YouTube. He typed into the search bar "how to make money online". He saw a few videos pop up that grabbed his attention and noticed many of these videos had a description right below the video.

When he clicked on the description, it would take him to a landing page (a web page where you can enter your email address in exchange for something like a free report or video for example). You get on somebody's email list and then they can send you emails with some offers.

He noticed these people were getting a ton of free traffic. John decided right then that he would master YouTube – and that's exactly what he did.

After months of struggle, and literally one week before he was completely broke, he got his first $250 sale!

After having tried so many things that haven't worked, it finally it worked out! From that point, he focused on uploading more and more videos on YouTube. Before he knew it, within 4 months, he reached his first $10,000 a month thanks to offering affiliate products through his YouTube videos.

I asked John how he felt. He said it was crazy – like winning the lottery – yet more... because the lottery you just win it, but in his case he had put a lot of time, effort, and risked everything.

Everyday he had been in front of his computer trying to figure things out until 4:00 in the morning. His wife was pregnant and at home at that time, was expecting a baby soon and he had no income coming in, so it was really tough.

How John Turned $80 into $20,000

His first $250 sale came from an affiliate offer. What he did was include a link to a landing page in the description of his video, and when somebody opted in, they would see the offer and if they bought, John would get $250.

He saw the video worked, the landing page worked, the offer worked, so all he did was do more of that. It was simply a matter of scaling up now.

Initially, he re-uploaded that video multiple times and that one video that somebody on Fiverr created for him for $80 generated a total of about $15,000-$20,000.

Living the Freedom Lifestyle Thanks to YouTube

Freedom was the number one thing that John got as a result of his success on YouTube. He doesn't have a boss on top of his head and has free time to do anything he wants. He gets to go to the beach everyday. He's his own boss and can work from home or from his laptop where he can take his family and go anywhere in the world. All he needs to do is open his laptop and he's back in business.

Before, he would literally see his kid only in pictures because of the long hours he was working – leaving early in the morning and coming back late at night. In John's own words, this lifestyle has given him "Freedom, freedom, freedom. For me, that's what it was all about, freedom."

How to Get Targeted Buyers Traffic from YouTube

There are many ways to earn money from your channel. You can earn affiliate commissions by reviewing products, or you can redirect this traffic instead to your landing page, build an email list, and promote whatever you want.

Tip: Product reviews are a good way to get highly targeted buyers traffic because people who are looking for products, especially business opportunity seekers, are looking for reviews to see if it's legitimate. These people are holding a credit card and are ready to buy, but want to confirm if the product is any good before they make the purchase.

It's easy to create videos for product reviews because there are so many products launched every single day.

Initially, what John focuses on ranking for is YouTube, but once a video becomes very popular on YouTube and is ranking well, then he starts to focus on ranking it on Google.

To get a video on the first page of Google, apart from the optimized content and keywords, what you need is what are called "backlinks". Basically, backlinks are links pointing from different places on the web to your video.

Getting backlinks is a signal to Google that you're relevant. Think of it as a vote of confidence.

You'll need quite a few different kinds of backlinks constantly feeding that video and eventually when the video starts getting very popular on YouTube, it can rank easily on Google as well.

It depends on the competition. You might rank straight away, because Google gives priority to videos, especially when it's a how-to video. It may take some time for the video to get found by Google first, before it's ranked.

John mainly uses Fiverr.com to buy backlinks, but he also uses SEOClerks.com. To make sure they're not the "spammy" low quality backlinks that could hurt his SEO, he tests a lot of backlink providers.

Important: *When you test new backlinks, don't mix new back-link sellers for a new video, so you can see if their backlinks are effective or not.*

If he finds that these new backlinks harms his video, then he blacklists that provider and never orders it again. He's now got a handful of trusted sellers that he does business with who help him to rank his videos.

If the channel or other videos gets bad links from a new provider on a new video, it would not affect any other video. If he has another video on the same channel that is ranking well, it's going to stay there and not be touched.

Whenever he orders backlinks, it's always only a handful and he's very careful what he's ordering. The strategies of spamming YouTube and Google with thousands of backlinks are dead; they don't work anymore and do more harm than good.

John also mentioned it's also good practice to build backlinks to your channel as well.

John's 70-year-old dad helps him to upload an average of 3 to 5 videos a day, depending on new product launches or the keywords that he provides him with, but at the minimum, 3 per day.

The type of videos vary and he does a bit of everything to always test what works best. Sometimes he's on camera, sometimes he gets someone on Fiverr to create whiteboard videos or do acting for him. It depends on the strategy he's using. These days, he creates more of his own videos and focuses on branding himself.

He also creates powerpoint presentations where he has a voice over along with text and images. It depends on your outcome. For example, if you're doing a product review and you're demonstrating the product (like software), then you might just record your screen.

To record his screen, John uses a screencast software (like camtasia PC/Mac or screenflow Mac). You can also record your webcam so it adds some personal connection as well and have it in the bottom right corner as you briefly go through the members area of the product and describe what's there.

How to Create Stunning YouTube Thumbnails

The video thumbnail is very important because that's how it attracts attention and gets the click. If it's just a boring picture, it won't attract the eye when people are scrolling down the results page.

He uses images from Google (Disclaimer: beware of using copyrighted images), and then edits them into thumbnails using Pixlr.com.

 Tip: *Make sure that the end thumbnail stands out with the right color and the right message. For example, if you look at the competition and let's say most of the thumbnails are blue, then you might pick a red one or similar.*

The One Thing You Must Do to Get Started Now

I asked John if there was one piece of advice that he would like to leave with you.

Take action. It's really simple. It's not complicated. What he sees from many people is they over-complicate things and they get analysis paralysis. In the end, they don't do anything.

Don't be afraid to make a video and be in front of the camera. It's not such a big deal. The more you do it, the better you become and the better results you will get.

If you absolutely don't want to be on camera, then you don't have to. There's always a way to do it even if you're not so good at talking.

At the end of the day, just take action.

Additional Content

 Watch the full exclusive YouTube VIP interview here: http://vidtr.in/john

CHAPTER **18**

Evan Carmichael: How to Get 497,930+ Subscribers on YouTube

Chapter Overview

In this interview, you'll learn how Evan went from entrepreneur to YouTuber who managed to grow his channel to over 497,930+ subscribers.

Connect With Evan

Website: www.evancarmichael.com

YouTube Channel: @ModelingTheMasters

Twitter: @EvanCarmichael
Facebook: @evan.carmichael

Before **Evan Carmichael** got into YouTube, he was an entrepreneur and had his own business when he was 19, built it up, and then sold it. He got asked to do a bunch of speaking and decided that he wanted to help other entrepreneurs who are going through the same issues that he had to go through.

Evan started off on his website where he was posting content regularly about his own thoughts and what he learned from famous entrepreneurs. That's when his YouTube channel started. His primary objective was he just wanted to share more – he loved entrepreneur stories because it saved his business.

He learned how Bill Gates started his software company and that helped him with his software company, so he wanted to share those lessons with other people. Since he was a visual learner, he would have rather seen videos rather than written articles, so that's when he created his channel.

Evan didn't have any aspirations to become a YouTube star, as it was just another way to be able to share some content. For example, when people started asking him questions, instead of writing an email response, which would have taken him a long time, he decided instead to make a YouTube video for that person and for anybody else who might have the same problem.

From Zero to 500,000

I asked Evan how long it took him to reach almost ½ a million subscribers. He remembers somebody was looking at the stats, it was about 8 years ago when he started on YouTube. The truth is, just like anything else when you start taking it more seriously, you're going to start creating more impact and start seeing better results.

About 2 years ago was when he started to really take it seriously and that's when he started making daily content instead of just once a week or whenever he felt like it.

So he eventually made the transition from treating it like a hobby that he was doing on the side, to something he's dedicating himself to and making it work.

The more work and effort he put in, the faster he got results.

From Camera Nervous to 9 Videos Per Day

Evan's biggest challenge at the start was not feeling super comfortable in front of the camera. It took him a while to get used to it and get comfortable. He used to only be able to film when he was by himself at the start, using his flip camera. He would put this camera on his cabinet and then just start filming.

Then he moved on to use a Nikon camera. The problem was it wouldn't focus automatically, so he would have to have someone on his team or his sister or wife come in and focus it for him, press record. Then he would have them leave the room and close the door because he couldn't do it with them in the room, he was too nervous – even though it was people who he knew wouldn't judge him.

This was one of the biggest hurdles at the start – overcoming the nerves, or the feeling of not knowing what he's going to say, thinking that the video isn't going to be good, and judging his own work.

 Tip: *If you're feeling nervous in front of the camera, the only way to overcome that feeling is to just do it anyway. What's helpful is to commit to filming at least 15 videos with the thought that you don't have to publish it if you don't want to.*

At the start, he was also doing everything himself. He was researching, filming, editing, being the guy on the camera, being the guy behind the scenes, posting to YouTube, titling, tagging, everything! That really slowed him down how much he could do especially when he had a business to run at the same time.

Then, as he started growing, he brought on a team. The first person he brought on was an editor and that allowed him to go to 1 video a day, instead of one video a week, which made a huge impact on what he was able to do previously.

Now he has 3 editors on the channel, and he's able to do 3-9 videos a day, every single day. It's a lot of content, but he's been able to scale up beyond himself so it's not just him doing everything.

> **Super Tip:** *You can hire a full time video editor in the Philippines for only $300 a month. This is just over the average wage ($279) of the population and will free up your time dramatically. You can find Philippine video editing outsourcers on Upwork.com. Make sure to ask for a portfolio to see their editing style. Why Philippines? They are very well educated, fluent in English, and have a strong work ethic.*

Would You Like a Dose of Entspresso?

The content he creates is really around what is interesting to him and what he wants to learn, so a huge chunk of it is around the famous entrepreneurs.

Basically, his process is this:

He thinks about who he wants to learn about, who the audience wants to hear about, and then he starts researching to find out something about that person who has a message.

What's really important for somebody who's getting started or who wants to model this approach, is to think about content that will be applicable to a wide audience and then narrow it down to be more specific.

For example, **Evan has three types of videos.**

He has the **Top 10 Rules For Success Series** that does really well. He's not really in it that much, he's just doing the intro and the outro at the end.

The next series he has is the **Entspresso Series** where it's half famous entrepreneur and half him, so the entrepreneur will say something about the theme of the day and then Evan will say something to add onto it.

Then the third kind of video is where it's all him where he shares his thoughts on something.

Hero Videos vs. Hygiene Videos

Having content that is interesting to a lot of people really helps. In the YouTube world, they call these the Hero Videos. There's actually two types: The Hero and The Hygiene. The Hygiene is the daily stuff and The Hero are the ones you put a ton of effort and love into to get a lot of attention.

It really helps to slowly introduce people to himself. They may not have heard of him, but they've heard of whatever topic he's covering or whatever famous entrepreneur he's talking about in the video. Then they're like "Who's this Evan Carmichael guy?" and they'll want to watch other videos he's putting out as well.

Almost all of the videos are a combination of requests from the audience and then something he's interested in.

All the Top 10s, Believe Lifes, and Entspressos are requests; most of the videos are requests from people who are interested in that entrepreneur. That entrepreneur must also interest Evan and also must have enough information to pull together to make a video on.

So it starts with the audience and what they care about, it'll then go to the research phase, he films it, his editor puts it all together, and then he posts it.

Evan's Simple Strategy to Get More Video Views

Every quarter, Evan sits down and thinks "How do I get the videos to take off more?". Even with almost ½ a million subscribers, he asks himself, "Why isn't it at 5 million subscribers?". He still has bigger ambitions than the results he has now.

So although promoting your video on Twitter, in your email newsletter, having a good title, thumbnail, and doing better SEO matters, all of those things will help you get ranked in the short term, but what YouTube cares a lot about is watch time. This is the most important ranking factor for YouTube.

If people are watching your videos, then they're going to recommend it much more often. To get more watch time has nothing to do with thumbnails, title, tags, description, or any of that stuff – it comes down to is your stuff any good? Do people want to sit there and watch your video, however long it is? Is it good enough?

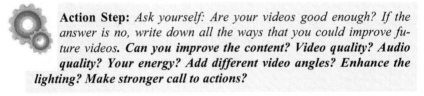

Action Step: *Ask yourself: Are your videos good enough? If the answer is no, write down all the ways that you could improve future videos.* ***Can you improve the content? Video quality? Audio quality? Your energy? Add different video angles? Enhance the lighting? Make stronger call to actions?***

This is the sobering truth because we'd like to think that it's easily solved by changing our titles, putting in new thumbnails, or whatever – yes, those things do matter, but much more important is just being better – having better content, having better footage, and putting more love into your videos.

Creating better content is still his challenge right now, even since the beginning. If you take a look at his thumbnails, they've gotten a lot better, same with the editing process. It's still got to come down to you getting better at what you do, whether you're a talking head on camera or if you're playing games or doing tutorials.

It's taken Evan 4,000 videos to get to where he is now, but he admits he still needs to get better. A marketing strategy isn't going to save him; he needs to make better videos!

How to Bring an Audience with You

Evan believes that you'll bring an audience with you. As people like your style, your message, and want to learn from you, whether you're entertaining them, educating them, or whatever style and content you're giving to them, people get used to it.

If you look at his community, it's one of the most positive communities out there where the comments are super positive and people are trying to encourage each other and help each other out. It's a reflection of that he spreads, because he's not spreading hate, negativity, or anger. That's why these types of people are attracted to him.

If you're really being who you are and being authentic, not just being a showman for your audience, then you'll start to attract the right audience to yourself. Yes, you do need to listen to them, but you also have to have a vision for where you want to go.

It's Not about the Laptop Lifestyle; It's about Doing What You Love Every Day

When I asked Evan about the type of lifestyle he's been able to live as a result of his YouTube success, I mistakenly assumed it was the "Laptop Lifestyle" many internet marketers and entrepreneurs dream about – sitting under the palm trees sipping piña coladas and working only a few hours a week.

His response was unexpected, but made complete sense to me and put it into a more down-to-earth perspective.

He said, "I don't live a lifestyle". If you're really serious about doing anything, then you're not living a laptop lifestyle. If you look at any of the top YouTubers, any of the people making 'huge bank' off YouTube, they're not living the laptop lifestyle. They're working hard!

He can work from a laptop anywhere in the world he wants to be and he looks forward doing videos and enjoys spending time with his community.

Evan does 2 streams every day, plus interview streams, plus his regular videos and then when he's not doing the videos, he's reviewing them, doing the research, thinking about how to grow the channel, or start a new video series.

He said he would die on the beach and after an afternoon would want to leave and go do something else, like thinking about his channel or another business idea.

It's good for people to find the thing that they love doing that other people see as torture but that they really can't wait to go back and do again.

When Evan goes travelling, he's filming. When he goes away speaking at an event or goes on a vacation, he brings his camera with him and he's filming. Even when he's sick, he's doing the videos and will be in front of the camera with a tea talking to his audience. He doesn't remember the last time he took a week off from his channel and doesn't see it as a burden, but something he loves to do.

 Tip: *Whenever you travel, make sure to bring your camera and video gear along so you can create content during your trip. It will give new context to your videos and make it more interesting for your subscribers to watch, with new backgrounds and different places.*

Test the Process before Committing

First of all, test it out and see if you like the process, not just the end result. If you're just chasing subscribers, you're never going to get there because you don't enjoy the work of doing the videos.

He enjoys playing League of Legends, so in the morning he'll do a League of Legends live stream where he plays the game and for an hour take business questions from his audience while he places.

It's all about finding what you can play and what you can love doing.

For him it was not the editing, he found out pretty quickly that he did not enjoy that process very much, so he needed to give that over to someone else to do.

Posting to YouTube, uploading the file, adding in the tags, and all that is not what he loves doing, but some people get off on that. For some people they love data and analytics. Whatever your thing is, you need to try to spend as much time doing that as possible and when you're first starting out and you don't have the capital to bring on a team yet, that's OK.

Maybe you're not spending 80% of your time on that thing, but you need to make sure you spend some time because a lot of people spend no time on the thing that they love doing or the thing that they could be the best in the world at. They're thinking and daydreaming about it, but they're not actually doing anything about it.

So if you want to have success on YouTube, it's not just because you see Pewdiepie (@PewDiePie) or whoever else doing really well. That's probably the worst reason to try to be a YouTuber. It's because you like making content, you like interacting with the audience, you like being on camera, you like making different kinds of videos... you have to enjoy the process.

Figure out what it is you love doing by trial and error – and see... you might make 5 videos and hate 80% of the process, but there's 20% that you really love. Then hone it on that 20% and figure out ways to do more and more of that.

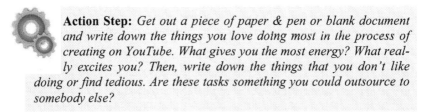

Action Step: *Get out a piece of paper & pen or blank document and write down the things you love doing most in the process of creating on YouTube. What gives you the most energy? What really excites you? Then, write down the things that you don't like doing or find tedious. Are these tasks something you could outsource to somebody else?*

Expect to Suck at First

If you're just starting out and at the beginning of your YouTube journey, expect to suck. This is what's really hard for a lot of people.

For example, let's say you want to teach dance on YouTube. Great! You can look at other dance channels and you see how great they are. Then you have this kind of standard for what you think a good video should be like. Maybe you feel you could do it way better than they do on the other channels, you know you're a better dancer than they are and know your stuff better than they do.

So you get on camera and it doesn't come out as you expect. You're nervous, you didn't get the right angle, didn't know how to do the effects or you didn't say the right thing. In other words, what you end up producing is not at the level that other people are doing, but you still feel like you could get there.

What a lot of people do at this point is quit, because they see that their thing sucks, they know it sucks, and it does suck! Your first anything sucks – your first time on a bicycle sucks, your first time on a snowboard sucks, the first time you did an interview you were probably super nervous and you sucked. What do you expect, it's your first time doing something!

People have unrealistic expectations where they think they're going to be great and then they suck and it's a total letdown and they never go back to it.

So if you go in, you still should have your dream of where you want to go and the belief that you can get there, but expect to suck at the start.

Additional Content

Watch the full exclusive YouTube VIP interview here:
http://vidtr.in/evan

CHAPTER 19

Andrii Pogorilyi: How to Earn $200,000 from Multiple YouTube Channels Thanks to SEO and Trending Topics

Chapter Overview

In this interview, you'll learn how Andrii earned over $200,000 from multiple YouTube channels by tapping into SEO strategies and trending topics.

Connect With Andrii

Website: www.ituber.me (Russian)

YouTube Channels:
"iTuber" (Russian)
"Voody Games" (@Predaindex) (Russian)
"Mr Gear"
Facebook: @andrew.pogoreliy

Andrii Pogorilyi has earned over $200,000 from three different YouTube channels using in-depth SEO and trending topics. He's also a YouTube certified audience growth expert.

Before he got started on YouTube, Andrii was a professional interpreter and had his own translation agency, which translated Chinese, Russian, and Ukrainian languages.

Eventually, he discovered YouTube and saw people uploading different kinds of videos. He found it interesting, but was not sure how he could monetize it, so he lost interest.

It wasn't long after that he saw that some people were sharing checks and earnings they've made from YouTube. He found that the first guys that were earning something on YouTube were gamers, uploading recordings of their games.

Since he already was into playing a lot of games in his spare time, he thought "Why not me?" So he decided to try it out himself.

5,000 to 10,000 Subscribers Per Day

It was then that the Voody Games channel was born. At the time of this publication, it had over 500,000 subscribers.

Andrii started to upload some games and record some of his list plays. It took him almost half a year of struggle to achieve 1,000 subscribers. During this stage, it was just a hobby for him.

After this initial period, the number of subscribers added to the channel grew larger and was gaining 5,000 to 10,000 subscribers per day. This was a defining moment for him and was the beginning of his success on YouTube.

He started to earn $5,000 to $25,000 per month by monetizing the views on his videos through the YouTube AdSense program. After that, some big worldwide brands appeared and gave him some proposals for products or reviews of games. He continues to work with these brands today.

One of the challenges that Andrii faced was when he first started his channel was that he only recorded games that he really enjoyed to play. The problem was, he wasn't thinking about what the market wanted to watch. As a result, he didn't get a lot of views or subscribers.

That's when he realized it's also about what the market likes. He decided to analyze the market and saw that people like some games better than others.

 Action Step: *Ask yourself: Are you sharing content that only appeals to you, or are you also thinking about what the market wants so you can serve more people?*

Quick SEO Tips from Andrii

Doing research on SEO really helped him to understand that it's important to help your audience to find your videos.

He discovered how to optimize the title, description, tags, and also how to make good subtitles. Subtitles (closed captions) are really important for SEO as well, so make sure to include closed captioning in your videos.

Creating and optimizing playlists can also help you to get found in the search results. After SEO research, he has a look at the content side of things and looks for trending themes.

Tip: *To find trending topics and themes, go to trends.google.com and do a search with a keyword. You can see if and when that keyword phrase started gaining popularity. You can also look at the topics key influencers on YouTube are already covering and model those videos. If it's popular on another channel, it has a chance to be popular on yours.*

After applying all these things, he got really great results – his videos were on the home page, others were sharing them, and they were all over the Internet.

How to Create More Engaging Videos That Get Higher Retention Views

In Russia, they have a website called Yandex - it's the main search engine there just like Google is in the majority of the world. He used the keyword tool and various plugins to find the right text and keywords. It also helped him to find trending videos and topics. He used Google Trends to find which topics are more popular than others and chose the most popular ones to make his videos.

Once he uploaded the videos, he analyzed them with YouTube analytics. There are some charts that show which moments of your videos are better viewed and which parts are less viewed. What you want to do is discover for yourself what you can cut into and include again in the next video to keep viewers engaged.

Super Tip: *If you go into your Creator Studio dashboard under Analytics -> Audience Retention, you'll see a graph for both absolute and relative audience retention. This allows you to see where viewers drop off in the video.*

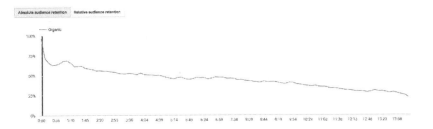

From his experience, it's very good practice to add the best or most shocking moment of your video at the start of your video, even just two or three seconds, to get people's attention and make them think "What was that? It was really unexpected, interesting, and amazing!".

This moment will "hook" them and they will continue to watch your video. If they like it, they will subscribe and click the share & like button.

Russian YouTube Pays Less?!

Andrii's experience with YouTube AdSense in Russia was that they pay much less than in Western countries. He gets between $1-5 CPM (cost per mil = per thousand views).

His second channel called "MrGear" is the most popular life hacks channel in the world. It's a worldwide channel without words and gets a lot of traffic from USA and Canada, so the countries where the monetization is really high. He makes most of his money from YouTube ads on this channel.

On his "Voody Games" channel, he uses sponsorship from brands as his main form of monetization. He makes some videos for them or reviews their games.

On his third channel called "iTuber", he uses a different type of monetization. This is an educational channel about YouTube and similar topics where he creates tutorial videos. He has completely disabled advert monetization.

Instead, he has a link in the description of the videos that point them to a landing page with a report they can download to learn more about YouTube in exchange for their name and email.

Action Step: *Think about what kind of free content with high-perceived value you can provide for your audience in exchange for their details. It doesn't have to be long, even a 3-5 page report will be enough. As long as the information is valuable and useful to the reader that's what counts. Even better is if they can start seeing results right away when they apply it.*

Once they're on his list, he sends them some emails and introduces them to his products about YouTube, educational books on Amazon, and other affiliate products. This type of monetization best suits people like coaches and trainers.

How Andrii Bought a New Car, a New Home, and Went on Holiday for Three Months Thanks to YouTube

I asked Andrii what kind of lifestyle he's been able to live because of his success on YouTube.

Before YouTube, he was a businessman, working long hours without any vacations, and very little sleep.

When he started his YouTube channel and got a lot of income, he had the choice to buy a new car, live in a new home, and go on holiday for three months, for the first time in his life.

Now he has the choice to go wherever he wants, to live wherever he wants, and eats food wherever he wants. He lives the good life, and drives nice cars.

"YouTube really changes people's lives."

Tips on Starting a Brand New Channel

1) The first step if you're just starting out or have a small channel is focus on SEO. There are a lot of tutorials and videos about how to do YouTube SEO. Just go to YouTube and type in how to optimize videos on YouTube.

2) The second step is to make videos about topics that are trending. If people want to know about something really bad, they want a lot of content about this topic. Just give it to them.

   Andrii's seen a lot of channels that grew very fast because they were making different videos, without much result – but then they just made one, short video about a topic that is trending and their channel exploded in growth – a ton of views, subscribers, and income.

   Be sure to react on trends. For example, today we have some worldwide trends like Trump becoming president. You could make a video about that. You'll get some views and traffic from this current trending topic. Just try it.

3) The third thing is don't be afraid to show your face and yourself on camera. People subscribe to other people, not to channels.

From his experience, people want to see another person, want to connect with them and be friends with them. They want to share their thoughts with that person.

When you're on camera, be friendly, be yourself. Show yourself on the camera from the start and don't be shy. Don't be afraid of that because there are a lot of YouTubers who are fat, thin, or have some other imperfections. Even Andrii has body concerns, but they're not a problem for his audience.

Important: *People connect with people. Being in front of the camera creates a stronger bond with your audience than if you're just talking over recorded slides or animations.*

The important thing is considering how can you communicate with them? Can you be a friend for your audience? Can you share some experiences from your life with them? Can you give them some exclusive content that they can't find on other channels? Be unique and be friendly!

Additional Content

Watch the full exclusive YouTube VIP interview here:
http://vidtr.in/andrii

CHAPTER 20

Stoica Bogdan: How to Use Software to Reverse Engineer YouTube's Ranking Algorithm

Chapter Overview

In this interview, you'll learn how Stoica helped develop software that automatically generates the perfect video details for maximum ranking potential.

Connect With Stoica

Website: http://vidtr.in/vmb

Facebook: http://vidtr.in/stoicafb

I t was about one month into my YouTube journey when I discovered the software (vidtr.in/vmb) that would help me rank for virtually any keyword I wanted. When I started using it, I was fascinated because the creators claimed they had "reverse engineered" the YouTube algorithm.

 Tools & Resources:

Video Marketing Blaster - vidtr.in/vmb

This is the software that Stoica helped develop, which auto-generates the title, description, and tags for your video, helping it to rank really easily.

From Programmer to YouTube Marketer

Stoica Bogdan got into YouTube about 9 years ago, but not in the normal way that most do. Before he started using the platform, he and his partner Vlad were developing and programming games since they were in 9th grade.

During this time, they found out about the Freelancer.com website and started to develop software for clients. They started to get more gigs from Internet marketing tools and were baffled about how they could afford to pay them big bucks for these projects.

Curiosity took over and Stoica and his business partner started to see what they're using the software for. That's when they first found out about YouTube marketing. So they started creating their own software for YouTube after experimenting, found the best methods and automated them.

Reverse Engineering the YouTube Ranking Algorithm

Since they were on YouTube from the early beginning, they had the privilege to see each update YouTube made to its algorithm and had time to try to understand and figure out how it ranks the videos.

9 years ago when they started, it was enough to just enter the keyword as many times as you were able to in the description and title and "BANG!", you were the first result for that keyword.

Next, YouTube started to look the age of the account to determine how to rank the videos. If the video was older, it got an unfair advantage in the rankings. During that period, Stoica and Vlad were uploading tons of videos as "unlisted" for upcoming events that they knew would be coming up in 6 months time.

6 months later, they made the videos public, and sure enough, they were the oldest result on YouTube for that keyword and were always top ranking.

Before they developed the software, YouTube did another major update, so they figured that they have to test each and every thing out to see what does and doesn't matter in the ranking algorithm.

During the software tests, they uploaded over 10,000 videos to test different things out, through split testing and similar methods.

Stoica said that they always keep their tools updated to the latest changes on YouTube, and since their YouTube tool was launched 5 years ago, it already has over 200 updates already.

His partner Vlad is working with him in the office and every day, they release a new update for one of their 10 tools. They always are making sure their clients can take advantage of the newest and most powerful YouTube features.

One of the challenges that Stoica faced was that YouTube was favoring the old accounts and old videos, so it was really hard for them to create tests and try to rank for, say, "Weight Loss". YouTube was giving authority only to videos that were 4 years old, for example, so they couldn't realistically make a test and wait four years to see if they set up all the elements correctly.

This became a problem not only for Stoica, but for others as well. YouTube started to have only old results for the top keywords and they started to realize that, for example in weight loss, maybe the recipes or programs that worked 6 years ago are now outdated and there were better solutions available.

This was a huge problem, but thankfully, YouTube decided to change that and Stoica and his partner were able to continue testing.

How One Of His Clients Gets 300,000 Views On Videos In Romania

When Stoica first started on YouTube, he was in semi-blackhat niches like movies, TV series, trailers, etc. He and his clients all had channels with millions of views. It was an easy niche to be in, but was unsustainable.

They soon decided to move out of this niche because of all the copyright claims that prevented them from creating steady income streams on their channels, which got shut down.

Stoica and Vlad had a lot of clients that they helped to create an account from scratch. For example, they had a friend and client in their city that came and asked them if they could help him to create a weight loss channel to share his story.

If you search in Romanian "weight loss exercises" or similar hardcore keywords like this one, his channel and videos are the first to come up. He has videos with 200,000-300,000 views in a pretty small niche and country like Romania.

I asked Stoica how his lifestyle is as a result of his success with his Internet marketing software business.

The lifestyle is pretty cool because when all of his colleagues and friends are at work, and you stay home or are in a café getting a coffee and you call them and say "Hey man, can you come and grab a coffee with me?" and they're like "Oh no, I'm at work", you feel pretty good and you feel happy about your life. Also, you can earn 10x or more what they are doing from 9-5.

How the Software Works

The application allows you to find untapped keywords, analyzes your competition, and automatically creates the perfect SEO titles, descriptions, and tags. All these three things work together, even if in the software you see them in three different modules, the software is doing the whole process at once.

It needs to analyze the competition to create the titles and descriptions, and in order to create those, it needs to find keywords that are related to your main keyword.

Nine years ago, it was OK just to repeat the exact keyword ten times in the description. That doesn't work anymore. Now you have to use related keywords and lexical semantic keywords (keyword phrases that mean the same, but are a variation of the main keyword).

So the software basically finds these similar keywords that helps your video rank for the main keyword. That's how the elements are generated.

Super Tip: *To find related and lexical semantic keywords, you can use the Google Keyword Planner tool by entering the main keyword and then looking at the related keyword ideas that come up. You can also look for key phrases that are used in the descriptions of the top ranking videos on YouTube for your keyword and incorporate them into your video description.*

How to Discover YouTube Keywords' Search Volume

Don't go after keywords with high volume. Why? Because everybody will fight to rank for example "Plumber Florida". If you try to rank for this, there might be 100 other marketers who try to target that keyword. It will be really hard for you.

Important: *Look for long tail keyword phrases and also for keywords that show buyer intent if you want to generate the most sales from your YouTube traffic.*

Instead, he recommends checking out the best keywords in the software that are less competitive, for example "Emergency Plumber Florida". This would be a good keyword because if somebody has an emergency, he will pay no matter what the cost to get it fixed, so you'll actually get more clients, even if you just get 5 views versus 50 views that are not as targeted.

Since YouTube doesn't have a dedicated keyword research tool like Google does, it can be more difficult to figure out how much search traffic a keyword has. This is actually a good thing, because the less people know about how much search volume a keyword has, the less competition there is for those keywords.

Stoica's advice is don't target high competition keywords. Just think outside the box.

You don't have to rank or build your whole channel around for example "weight loss". That's too broad. Instead, target keywords like "weight loss for office workers". Even if you get 10% of the traffic that you would get ranking for "weight loss", it will be much easier to rank for and you will get way more targeted traffic.

Additional Content

Watch the full exclusive YouTube VIP interview here: http://vidtr.in/stoica

Download the software here: http://vidtr.in/vmb

CHAPTER **21**

Antonio Centeno:
How to Make $100,000 per
Year from YouTube

Chapter Overview

In this interview, you'll learn how Antonio went from being a clothier to making over $100,000 a year from YouTube which now allows him the freedom to travel anywhere in the world for as long as he wants.

Connect With Antonio

Website: www.realmenrealstyle.com

YouTube Channel:
@RealMenRealStyle

Twitter: @RMRStyle
Facebook: @RealMenRealStyle

I came across **Antonio Centeno**'s channel when I was searching "how I made $100,000 on YouTube" and his video was in the first position.

From U.S. Marine Officer to Clothier to YouTube Star

Before Antonio started his YouTube channel, he was an officer in the U.S. Marines Corps for 5 years. After that, he went to business school for a couple of years to figure out business for himself.

Soon after, he started a custom clothier and from that, he created his YouTube channel, for the main purpose of a marketing channel.

He approached YouTube as a businessman – to try to get more traffic to his website. Antonio figured out that there was less competition and was the best option because he couldn't afford a marketing or PR firm at the time.

He knew what he was talking about, and there wasn't anyone else talking about this niche in the way he was talking about it, so he believed he could enter the wide open "blue ocean" where he could go in and be able to dominate the niche within a few years if he created some decent content.

It was 2012 when he started going hard on YouTube. Before that, he was only uploading a few videos here and there, but didn't really do much.

In 2012, he created 200 videos in 200 days. It sounds like a lot, but initially, he set the goal of 10 videos in 10 days. He didn't shoot every video every single day. Instead, he did a batch process, so there were days where he would film 10 videos in a day. His record was 20 videos in a single day.

To shoot the videos, all he did was sit in front of the camera, hit record, and talk about what he already knew. He didn't do any edits, so a video only took 10 minutes to shoot and he could get quite a few done in an afternoon.

In his opinion, his early videos kind of suck, but still to this day people still comment on them and give him feedback.

In his videos now, he implements this feedback, but at the time, he didn't know if his YouTube channel would actually work out and so didn't want to invest any time and money into it except for what he could to film the first set of videos. Every time he filmed, he always approached it with this question: "Are we going to get a return on investment on this?"

 Super Tip: *An interesting strategy is to go on your competitors' videos, go through viewers' comments and see if you can implement some of their feedback in your videos. This will immediately give you a competitive edge because you now have something your competitor does not that your audience wants.*

How Antonio Earns $10,000 for Advertising on YouTube Videos

Antonio's strategy was always about sales. At the end of the day, as a small business, he has to get sales. If he didn't, he wasn't going to stay in business. That was goal... but soon, the strategy shifted...

Antonio soon realized that it was a lot less competition and easier to make money, not so in the clothing, but selling either advertising space or selling his own information products.

Initially, he started with e-books and then went to courses. After courses, he started getting 5,000 people watching a video within about a 24-hour period.

Antonio realized that a lot of advertisers would pay for him to talk about their clothing. In fact, they actually approached him very early on, giving him a load of free products to review. The issue was it just took a lot of time to put these reviews together and he decided he wanted to charge for it instead.

He remembers the first time he did it, he charged a couple thousand dollars and he was very nervous about asking for that money, but then once he set that bar, it became normal. Nowadays, people pay him $10,000 to advertise on one of his videos. He's now reached the point where advertising is a big revenue source for him.

The key point is that he's not dependent on this – he monetizes his channel in 20 different ways now. It used to be when he owned the clothier, it was all about the clothing sales and he would have a great month and then a bad month.

Now, he can have a bad month with, for example, advertising but he'll make it up with affiliate sales, his own product sales, consulting, or other streams of revenue.

Consistently Create Good Content

I asked Antonio what his biggest challenge was during his YouTube journey. He responded by saying that the challenge shifts every year, but the biggest challenge was in being able to consistently create good content.

The problem is you can easily work 70-80 hours trying to run your business while creating your YouTube channel, but since he values spending time with this family, he had to find a solution.

To do that, he ended up hiring a videographer. He pays him for 20 video "credits" each month. If he doesn't use those 20 credits, it's like wasting his money. He started using this system about 2 years ago and has since been able to consistently produce at least 3 videos per week, because he doesn't have to edit the videos anymore.

He remembers the first 300 videos he had to edit, so there were weeks where he would go without putting out any videos, simply because he was busy with other things.

Since hiring his dedicated video guy, he's been able to produce videos consistently and the quality of them has continuously moved up.

In general, his channel views on a typical day when from around 20,000 per day to over 100,000 views per day on all of his videos across the channel.

How Antonio Got a Million Views on His Channel

It's important to note that Antonio never really had any viral videos. He mostly had videos that were well optimized, for example "how to tuck in a shirt". Those videos have consistently provided the traffic.

He came to the realization one day that he could get to a million views in a wide variety of ways. If he consistently got 1,000 views on every video he put out, then he'd just have to put out 1,000 videos. It's not ideal, but it definitely works!

As a result, he ended up getting more than an average of 1,000 views per video, so around video number 200, he hit a million views.

It's kind of like a snowball – it takes a lot of work in the beginning, but you'll start to see the right progress and indicators, and see everything move up.

He admits that he's still not the biggest channel in his space, which is fine, because you don't have to be the biggest to be able to create a profitable and successful YouTube business.

The key thing is not only being different and unique, but to really be useful and solve a problem and then people are going to seek you out.

Imagine Going on a 5-Month Trip and Making a Passive Income

Antonio's ability and capacity of freedom that his YouTube business affords him is inspiring. Although he says it took a while to get to where is now, he progressively moved up to it.

At the time of writing this, he was on a 5-month trip with his family. You can do this with a number of businesses, but the key with an online business is you can do it from anywhere.

He has around 12 people on his team and they're all over the world, so they're not going to notice anything different if he's on a half a year trip. This didn't come automatically though.

He worked to build up a lot of autonomy in his team so that if he doesn't talk with them for a week, they're fine. They know the direction that they can go.

That being said, he still has key performance indicators (KPIs) that they need to stick to. He knows that some of the things won't get done that he wanted to get done, but everything that needed to get done will get completed because everyone on his team owns their own particular niche in the business.

For example on social media, he doesn't spend any time. He has a Facebook page with over 80,000 likes and he has people that manage all that for him.

Entertain, Educate, and Motivate

If you are brand new on YouTube and just starting out, Antonio recommends studying and learning everything you can about YouTube marketing.

There's a guy called Tim Schmoyer at Video Creators (@VideoCreatorsTV) and he's got 200-300 videos that are really useful on how to build up a channel. The information is already out there, but most people aren't following best practices.

A lot of people start a channel and they wonder why nobody is beating down the door to watch it. It's really because they're not doing these three things: it needs to **entertain**, **educate**, or **motivate**. Ideally, you're doing all three of those.

His friend and business partner Aaron Marino (@AlphaMconsulting) is the biggest channel in his space because he does all three of those. Antonio said he tries to do all three, but he admits he's not the best entertainer. Aaron is a better entertainer than him, which is why he gets better views, but Antonio is a better educator, hence why he attracts a different type of advertiser than he does.

Aaron has no problem creating a video on teaching you how to shave your balls. Antonio wouldn't create that kind of video; that's not what he built. He'd rather do something like "The Science of Style". So he focuses on and uses his own strengths.

 Action Step: *Ask yourself: are your videos entertaining? Are they educational? Are they motivational? If the answer is no for any of these, then ask yourself how you can improve that aspect in future videos.*

How Becoming Friends with Your Competitors Will Lead to More Money

Antonio and Aaron partnered up to create a conference to bring together all of the people in their industry. Many people view them as main competitors to each other but they're not – and from that they created another company that's called "Menfluential", which is a media company.

Both of them get lots of people that contact them that want to advertise or say they want to work with them. The fact is, of that, only 10%, maybe 5% are serious, meaning that they're willing to spend money or are even within their budgets.

But because they brought together everyone in the industry by building their network and reaching out to people on YouTube in their industry, what they can do is farm that out to other people who are very thankful because their channel is very small.

For example, if someone only has $1,000 to advertise with, that's not enough to work with him. Instead, it works out well for everyone, because they're able to take a percentage of that, the creator is very happy because he gets something that he wouldn't have gotten, and the advertiser is happy because they get their advertising slot they were directed to.

To attract these types of opportunities, don't view these people that are ahead of you as competitors (they still are in a way) – but as friends or peers who push and help each other to become better.

Action Step: *Reach out to at least 10 channels in your niche and let them know that you'd like to collaborate with them and build up a long-term mutually beneficial relationship. Offer to help them in ways you see that their channel needs most help. Give them some tips if you see they need it. This will open up the door to opportunities in the future.*

Commit to at Least 25-50 Videos

A lot of people just start creating videos and they don't think of how they can actually build this out as a channel.

That's why Antonio recommends when you get started, just commit to at least 25-50 videos, which may seem like a lot to many people. He did 10 videos in 10 days, so you can easily do 100 videos in 100 days if you're willing to compromise at first.

You don't have to put out your best content first. Just solve that burning problem. When he was solving the burning problem in the fashion industry, he simply talked to the video camera, didn't show any examples, and the color wasn't great. It was the best he could do at the time, but what was important was he went into detail to address their problems.

CHAPTER 22

Roberto Blake: How to Go from 0 to 100,000+ Subscribers & Build a 6-Figure Business Thanks to YouTube

Chapter Overview

In this interview, you'll learn how Roberto went from being a creative services professional in an agency to building a 6-figure a year business thanks to growing his YouTube channel to over 100,000 subscribers.

Connect With Roberto

Website: www.robertoblake.com

YouTube Channel: https://www.youtube.com/user/robertoblake2

Facebook: https://www.facebook.com/robertoblake2/

Twitter: https://twitter.com/robertoblake

B efore he got into YouTube, **Roberto Blake** started out developing his corporate career, working in the creative services profession, which included graphic design, web design, SEO, marketing, and advertising.

He worked for an agency in midtown Manhattan doing billboard designs that were in Times Square. As a graphic designer, he knew a lot about visual branding and brand development.

He was also Google AdWords certified and knew how search engine marketing worked.

Roberto had been a freelance photographer since high school and college, but he'd also been doing video editing since he was 15 years old in the late 90s. He used to be an assistant photographer and videographer in a wedding business beforehand.

When he came to the YouTube platform, he was already coming with experience with what it was like to work with entrepreneurs and small businesses doing B2C and B2B client services. He was the guy in the companies he worked for who was teaching everyone their software, so it was a natural fit for him to start teaching these skills on YouTube.

He started his YouTube channel in 2009, but only started taking it seriously in 2013. Roberto believes that "You can't really claim to do something or be a YouTuber until you are taking it seriously and you are committed."

Do Not Obsess Over Subscribers

The thing most YouTubers obsess over wrongly is the subscriber count. Instead, it's better to obsess over the one thing you can control which is making your videos better. Focus on making the audio better, say less "ums" and "ahs", improve your cadence, and polish your on camera personality.

"All I was obsessing over was making my videos suck less. I was happy that if no one was watching, because I didn't think I had anything that was really great or polished yet."

"I think the info I was putting out was spot on & well presented and people agreed and they were learning from it. I felt I had so much room to improve that I didn't give a crap if no one was watching because I still had a ways to go before I could command their attention and deserve it in my opinion."

 Important: When you create a video, you're essentially asking for somebody's time out of their day, so make sure you're delivering real value and making their time worthwhile.

"I was asking people to spend 15 minutes learning Photoshop with me instead of making out with their girlfriend or boyfriend, that's a pretty big ask."

When Did You Start Thinking of Monetizing Your Channel & Turning It Into a Real Business?

"I started thinking about it from the beginning because by doing the tutorials, I was showing my skill set".

At the time, Roberto's concentration of his business was still in freelance design and creative services, but trying to bring this to the small business clients instead of agencies.

He was getting clients from his channel from the beginning because they would reach out to him and wanted him to do work for them.

Roberto made a bit of money from YouTube ads, but it was insignificant in the beginning because he was getting very little views.

The majority of his income from YouTube comes from the business that he generates from YouTube as a marketing channel.

"It's my best overall marketing channel and platform but I still have tens of thousands of followers outside of YouTube in other social media platforms. I still have a pretty significant email list that's almost 10,000 subscribers of an email list."

 Tip: *Even having a few thousand people on an email list can make you more money because you have direct access to their inbox.*

He used it to build a real business that he can scale up, so that if one day if YouTube ever does disappear, his business would hardly be affected.

That's why his personal brand is able to attract $5,000 to $10,000 speaking engagements and workshops. It means that he has credibility beyond YouTube, in video marketing. It's also why he never limits himself to YouTube and why he doesn't sell himself on being a YouTuber.

"I'm a video marketing practitioner. I'm someone who has shot, produced and edited and marketed over a thousand pieces of video content on the Internet."

"I've used it to make myself and other brands and businesses money. I can sell that, whether YouTube goes away or not, because there will always still be Facebook, Instagram, Twitter and live streaming."

How To Get Paid To Get Better At Editing Videos

A practical way to start making money while you are doing your own content is to find YouTubers who are looking for editors, freelance editors, and remote editors.

If you are doing "talking head" style content, which most of the YouTube videos are, then the reality is that it might not take you more than 15-30 minutes to edit somebody's 5 minute YouTube video.

This may not sound like a lot of money to some people, especially professional video editors, but if you're just starting out with video editing, then you could charge a YouTuber anywhere from $15-30 to edit their video for them. If they're already making money on YouTube, then this is a steal for them.

 Action Step: *Find someone with 50,000 to 200,000 subscribers that's making money on YouTube but has a lot of other stuff going on and wants to take editing off of their to do list.*

If it takes 30 minutes to edit a video and you get 6 videos edit, then you could be making a couple hundred dollars in a few hours.

A lot of people work a 9-5 job where after taxes they're not even clearing $60 for a full day of work.

Since you want to become a YouTuber anyways, then you might as well earn money as you get faster at editing anyway.

"If you want to quit your day job with YouTube, my answer is don't worry about making your money in YouTube AdSense, don't worry about trying to get so many subscribers and get a sponsor deal. Start editing videos for people and making money."

Affiliate Marketing On YouTube

Roberto also monetizes his channel with affiliate products. In his case because he's also a web designer, he could promote web hosting. The affiliate payouts are really good for web hosting, starting from $60 per sale of the lowest priced plans of $5/month.

Amazon is great for finding things that fit your niche, but the commission rate is only 4% starting based on volume.

Roberto gets around 8% commission now because he moves a couple of hundred units of product through Amazon and moves high-end gear like laptops.

If he sells a laptop through a laptop review via Amazon or on a buyer's guide on best laptops for 2017, then the reality is that a $600 laptop makes him the same as a $2,000 laptop because there is a cap limit put in place.

Find affiliate programs for other products that you're already using. For example, Roberto promoted TubeBuddy through an affiliate and sponsorship relationship.

"Just find for your niche what makes sense from a business standpoint. Look at the people, look at the ads that run on your YouTube channel, and start investigating those companies. Look at the things that you use day in and day out in what you do. I think that affiliate marketing lends itself very much to tech related channels like mine, to travel, to beauty, and to lifestyle. If you fit in any of those things I think it's practical."

Roberto's Biggest Challenge

The biggest challenge Roberto faced as he was building up his channel was **consistency**. The solution was simple: suck it up and be disciplined.

As to how much content you should create, it's different for everyone.

"It will be easy for me to say, 'Oh yeah put out as much content as possible, go to seven days a week like I did, here is how you do it.' I could tell you how to do that but it may not be practical."

"If I had kids there is no way I would do that unless I was hiring people to do the production and editing. There is no way I would do that to the degree and put out the level of content and the frequency of content that I currently do if I had kids or if I was married. That wouldn't be respecting my life and my relationships and the other people in my life."

"You have to figure out and be self-aware enough to accept that there will be things you can and cannot do based on who you are. If I had an illness of any kind there is no way I could do that kind of output."

Tip: *You have to do as much as is practical for your lifestyle and your situation. If you want to do more content, then find a way to make it work. You have to either get better at doing certain things or become faster at them or you might have to scale down the fancy stuff that you might think is necessary.*

How To Scale Up Your YouTube Channel

The YouTube algorithm favors frequency and view velocity. Daily videos are a great way to fulfill those factors, if you have a very good understanding of your niche.

Super Tip: *If you have a niche, daily content will escalate you in YouTube faster than anything, but you will have to do daily content for three to six months to a year for that to really take hold.*

You can't just do daily content for a month and say, 'Oh, I guess daily content doesn't work.' You really need to give it more time.

"I have to be real with you about that, it's a hundred days. If you really want to know if something is working in YouTube, it's hundred day cycles before reset, that's a programmer thing."

"I worked with web developers, programmers and database engineers in corporate long enough and I have to hire these people for certain things and I talk to them and some of them consult."

"I still have friends that are deep into the web master and web development community and it's not that I'm getting this from YouTube engineers, but I looked at the Google search engine and I've read Matt Cutts' blog. I know how Google as the parent company handles search and YouTube is built on the backbone of that."

"It's how even if I only get 5,000 views on a video, I can be above a video that has a half million views in the results. That's how granular I look at the data and that's how much the SEO relevancy part of the algorithm matters."

How Roberto Siphons Views From Popular Videos

Roberto shared a success story where he was able to get views from other popular videos.

"A bunch of people started putting out videos around October surrounding making money online and passive income. Two of my videos blew up."

"I had one video that had 50,000 views, another video that had a 100,000 views. From October to today, one of them is at over half a million views and the other one is on its way, because a bunch of people started putting up these passive income and making money online videos for some reason in about September, October and their videos did very well."

"My video was the most relevant video related to their video, so I started siphoning views from that. Also, I already knew that there was a spike in search around that topic and a spike in viewership around that topic."

"YouTube started serving those two videos and a few of my other ones on people's homepage more. That is because I optimized the hell out of those videos for search and they did well on their own."

Think Like a "BizTuber"

A BizTuber is a YouTuber who use YouTube, not as a destination, but as a vehicle. Roberto built his speaking career because of YouTube to get onto stages.

What the algorithm is doing is it not only cares about the views, but it cares more about watch time. In terms of how it markets and serves your videos, if it can't tie your video to other videos that someone watched, it has no user behavior association.

This means that if you watched 10 videos that were about online business, YouTube can't determine what videos to give you that are also related to online business so that it can keep you on the platform longer because of what you are currently interested in.

"Everyone complains about the algorithm but they are just not thinking about it logically as a buyer, they are not thinking about it as someone who is consuming video."

 Important: *The reason the upload frequency matters so much is because every day that you don't show up to relate to the new videos that just came out in your niche or topic to siphon views, is a missed opportunity.*

"It's not about whether your video goes viral. If someone else's video on the same topic goes viral, you will still siphon a percentage of those views based on related videos and on being served to the same viewership as them. Nobody is thinking about that."

How To Siphon Views Off Popular Videos

One of the things that is underutilized in YouTube are playlists. Most people only do a playlist of their own videos, which is fine. But not many people know that this is also a way to link your videos to other related videos, which allows you to siphon views from them.

If you cover a topic across multiple videos, then the best thing to do is to create a playlist:

1) Find a new way to phrase that topic and create a playlist title.
2) Write a description for the playlist just like you would for a video.
3) After, make your video the first in the playlist and then add a few more videos in that same topic.
4) Then add another video of yours. That way, all of a sudden there is a link between your videos and these other videos.
5) At the bottom of the description, link to other videos that cover the exact same topic, because now there will be an actual connection to those videos. This is a very smart and practical way to approach it.

With your video being the first one, if you tweet it out or you post it on Facebook, you are "stacking" watch time now because viewers will most likely watch the next videos in your playlist.

 Important: *The longer you keep someone on YouTube, the more authoritative your channel is.*

This is something people don't think about because most people think 'why would I promote other channels or videos that aren't mine?'. If you are the first thing in the thread, the credit goes to you and you are getting session watch time.

What people are not doing is they are not thinking of YouTube from the perspective of a viewer; they are not thinking like a fan.

If you think of YouTube as a client and you think about what's in YouTube's best interest, you start to realize that you need to adjust your strategy.

"What's in YouTube's best interest is keeping people on YouTube longer. What's in YouTube's best interest is watch time not just views. What's in YouTube's best interest is channels that are really good for advertisers and are advertiser friendly. What's good for YouTube is having more data to be able to let the robots do their job to distribute content."

"Especially if you are putting a lot of work into your videos and creating really great content, you want it to be exposed and you want to get out there and you want to rank."

"You have to give your stuff the best shot at success instead of hoping to have a magic bullet."

Don't Miss Your Opportunity For Greatness

So many people have so much fear and they are so determined to make YouTube their job that they miss an opportunity for greatness because they are too afraid to fail.

A lot of YouTubers today, even the successful ones, are not making great content, they are not taking risk anymore and they are not creating their best stuff because they are so afraid of looking bad.

"If you live your life catering to what other people want, you will be dissatisfied. They will all be satisfied and you will be the one left wanting because you have just been trying to please them. When you start living for yourself, they are going to complain because you are not serving them the way you used to."

"I think that you can do what you love in service to others on your own terms. That's what I do I help creative people, but I'm doing it on my own terms. If there is something that they want me to do that doesn't fit with who I am and what I want, I'm not doing it. I'm just not."

There is always someone else who can provide that value and they can go watch it over there and that's fine. You don't have to cry over it because there are people that you can help while doing what you love and doing the things that matter to you.

"While I'm on stage, sometimes there is 2,000, sometimes there is 500, and sometimes it's a bigger crowd than that."

"The value that they get and the difference it makes in their lives from those takeaways is often huge and sometimes is the difference between the success in their career or their business or their brand."

"I do one-on-one coaching consulting so I know that one person matters. If I make a video and it even gives one person a nugget, it's the same value as if I did a one-on-one consult. The numbers don't mean crap to me; people mean more than numbers."

Marques Brownlee also known as MKBHD (@marquesbrownlee) at over four million subscribers, one of the biggest tech YouTubers there is. He is one of the biggest YouTube success stories of all time, and has more influence over technology purchases than the New York Times. He works with almost every tech company in the world.

Did you know, on his first 100 videos he only got 78 subscribers. If you've done five videos, 10 videos, 30 videos, 50 videos and you are reading this, never whine about not getting subscribers. He had to do a hundred videos to not even get a hundred subscribers and he has four million today because he wasn't soft, he didn't quit, he didn't whine, he didn't give up, and he understood that a hundred people matter.

He did hundreds upon hundreds of hundreds of more videos about tech and the things he loved. He was able to not get into any kind of student loan debt, he was able to purchase a home and build an entire brand around doing what he loved on YouTube. All because a hundred videos of nobody watching didn't make him quit, didn't make him feel soft and didn't make him feel discouraged.

Having something where there was once nothing should be enough reason to keep creating. Every artist, illustrator, photographer, film maker 15 years ago had less people, less opportunities, and less people following them, and they still went on to do great and tremendous work. They would not say that it was a waste of time because they didn't get a thousand people to care about it.

"I have no respect for people who say, 'Well, I'm going to quit'; people who have like 10,000 subscribers, people who have 5,000 subscribers, people who have 1,000 subscribers and say, 'I'm not getting the views, or this isn't working or whatever or I can't sustain this so I'm just going to quit. I'm shutting the channel down, I'm deleting it or I'm just going to walk away.'"

"You are disrespecting hundreds of relationships. Even disrespecting dozens of relationships would be callous and would be a bad reflection of your character. If you can't you say, 'Well I can't do this full time', then don't do it full time. You know how many people do really cool stuff as a hobby day in and day out? You know how many great photographers and artists I know who don't make a living at it?"

"Just keep going and if you really enjoy doing it and making videos, then enjoy it and make videos whether you make a living at it or not."

"Also just something if any of you are artists out there tag me in your Instagram stuff. Tag me @robertoblake. I want to comment, I want to show you some love and I might do something with that later when I launch the new show."

"Remember everybody go out there and create something awesome today."

Additional Content

 Watch the full exclusive YouTube VIP interview here: http://vidtr.in/roberto

PART 4:
START YOUR JOURNEY

CHAPTER 23

Mindset Changes Everything!

Y our mindset will ultimately determine your success or failure on YouTube and every other area of your life. It's the one thing that separates the millionaires from the average Joes. The beautiful thing about it is, you can change it.

I cannot stress enough the power of this chapter, so if you're serious about creating lasting results, you must read and apply this information.

You may have found as you started to implement the strategies, that you have reached a point where you are stuck or aren't confident yet that you can achieve success. If so, this chapter will help ensure you have the right mindset and eliminate any mental or emotional blocks that could be holding you back.

I could give this book to 3 people with the exact same backgrounds, the same resources, and same education, yet each one of them will yield a different result.

One of them could get amazing success and make millions of dollars from applying these strategies. The other one could get mediocre results, and yet the third person could read the book, try the methods once and declare it doesn't work, or even call it a "scam".

Why is that, when the information in this book is exactly the same for all of them?

What Mindset Really Is

It comes down to **mindset**. When I talk about mindset, I don't mean the common knowledge definition that most people think as "positive thinking" or "believe and you will succeed" kind of things.

Yes, that does have its place, but I'm talking about your subconscious belief system, your core values and past conditioning that programmed you, how you think, and behave today.

Most people do not understand the power of their minds and believe that in order to change their results in their life, they just need to "act" differently. That is the wrong approach and will only lead to repeating the same patterns over and over again in different forms.

Einstein said that the definition of insanity is doing the same things over and over again, yet expecting a different result. You may "think" you're acting differently, but in reality, you're not. Let me illustrate...

We're going to work through this backwards...

What is behind your actions? Usually an emotion. Human behavior is largely driven by emotions.

What created or triggered that emotion? A thought or series of thoughts. How did those thoughts get created? By your existing thought patterns (inner environment) or outer environment such as the information you consume, the friends you spend time with, the country or area you live in, etc.

The Manifestation Process

Everything begins in your mind. Therefore, if you want to change your results in life, you must go to the root of the cause and change your thought patterns, belief system, core values, and conditioning.

This is how it works:

Belief System > Thoughts > Emotions > Actions > Results

The process starts from the invisible world (belief system, thoughts, emotions) and manifests in the visible world (actions and results).

Can you see how results can vary dramatically based on the different mindsets of people?

That's what separates the millionaires from the "wantrepreneurs" (the people who dream about being an entrepreneur, but never take action to become one or give up part-way).

We Have Two Minds

We have two minds: the conscious mind and the subconscious mind.

The conscious mind is the one you are aware of every day, while you're awake. Think of it as the "tip of the iceberg" in terms of its power and potential.

Another good analogy is the captain of a ship. It can steer your mind in the direction you want to go by using your willpower. It's the king of the kingdom of your body.

The subconscious mind is the mind you're not aware of, like when you're asleep, or when you've mastered a behavior and you perform it automatically, like driving a car. It's also where your thought patterns are stored and run mostly behind your conscious awareness. Think of it as the part of the "iceberg under the water".

Another good analogy is of the crew of a ship. The crew always listens and follows the orders of the captain (the conscious mind) if directed properly.

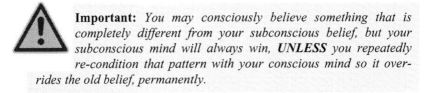

Important: *You may consciously believe something that is completely different from your subconscious belief, but your subconscious mind will always win,* **UNLESS** *you repeatedly re-condition that pattern with your conscious mind so it overrides the old belief, permanently.*

Here are a few methods that I've used to re-program my mindset for any outcome I want.

Model the Masters

As personal development guru Tony Robbins says, "Success leaves clues".

Every successful person has gotten to where they are by thinking a certain way, and then following a sequence of steps.

Instead of wasting years of your life trying to figure it out for yourself through costly trial and error, the smartest thing to do is model successful people.

Action Step: *In this case, if you want to become really good at creating YouTube videos and getting free targeted traffic from YouTube, study how the successful YouTubers are thinking.* ***What questions do they ask themselves? What is their mindset? What are they doing as a result of this mindset?***

Notice I didn't say just 'follow their strategy'. A strategy is a one-off thing and cannot account for the complexities of different situations that can come up along your journey. The only way to be nimble to be able to traverse these unexpected challenges is to **THINK** like these people.

Action Step: *Read their books, listen to their interviews, study their courses, even create a Hero board, where you print out their photo along with other people you admire and look up to, and put it where you look often. This will constantly impress and remind your subconscious mind to think, be and act like them.*

How to Eliminate Limiting Beliefs

Overcoming and eliminating limiting beliefs can be done in several different ways, but the end goal is the same – to re-program your neural pathways in a more empowering way.

Think of a belief as a filter where all the billions of bits of information your senses receive pass through. A belief is neither right nor wrong, it just is exactly the way you define it.

Anything that fits with your model of reality (your belief) is kept and is passed to your conscious mind, and everything else passes through undetected. Your subconscious mind will always try to make your outer reality congruent with your internal reality.

Let's say you have a subconscious limiting belief "Making money online is hard". So when you go to start an online business, you subconsciously choose strategies that are difficult or don't work.

You may try to sell a product that nobody wants. Then your conscious mind says, "See, I told you! Making money online is hard!"

You've just reinforced that belief...

Another example is if you apply some of the strategies in this book but stop taking action after 3 or 4 attempts if you don't see results right away.

Your conscious mind will "connect the dots" in the form of the subconscious belief blueprint you have and you'll say "See, I told you these YouTube strategies don't work, making money online IS hard!"

As Henry Ford said, "Whether you think you can, or you think you can't – you're right!"

Until you are aware of your limiting beliefs, you cannot change them.

Makes sense, right? You'd be surprised how many people try to "change" without first knowing what beliefs need changing. That's exactly like being in the dark trying to find the door to outside!

STEP 1: Become aware of your limiting beliefs

The first step is to ask yourself the following questions. Wherever there is a blank (_____) simply replace it with the area in your life you want to work on.

- What did I hear about _____ when I was growing up?
- What did my parents/teachers/elders say about _____ when I was a child?
- When it comes to _____, I feel angry because…
- When it comes to _____, I feel sad because…
- When it comes to _____, I feel frustrated because…
- When it comes to _____, I feel ashamed because…

These are a few questions that will help you start uncovering the automatic thought patterns that are lodged in your subconscious.

Write whatever thoughts come up, and don't filter them. For example:

When it comes to money, I feel frustrated because:

- I don't have enough of it
- It goes so fast
- Everyone wants it from me
- etc…

STEP 2: Inject doubt into existing limiting beliefs

Remember, a belief is just a thought that you feel a level of certainty about and is usually tied to a strong emotion. Your subconscious mind has neural association or "reference points" that support that belief and make it seem "true", even if it's far from it.

A good analogy of a belief is a multi-legged table. The top flat part of the table is the belief and the legs are all the other thoughts, life examples, other beliefs, and associations that keep it standing.

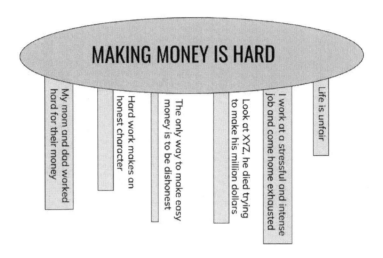

To weaken the belief, you must first inject doubt into it. To do this, all you need to do is reframe, change the meaning, or disprove the "legs", which will knock them out from under the "table".

For example:

To disprove "Hard work makes an honest character", I could point to an example in my life where I know a friend, family member, or role model who is wealthy and where money comes really easily to them, but they are still a very honest person.

Anything that you can come up with that makes fun of, disproves, and changes the statement will help.

Do this for all the "legs" and soon the "table" will have no supports and will crumble. Your limiting belief now has very little to no credibility.

STEP 3: Come up with a new empowering belief to replace the old limiting belief

Leaving the limiting belief in the crumbled state leaves a sort of space in your subconscious mind.

Think of it as a garden. You've weeded an area and there is now an empty patch of soil. If you would walk away now and return 2 weeks later, there will probably be the same weeds growing there again.

What you need to do is plant a new empowering belief there instead.

The next step is to come up with the opposite or more empowering belief. For example, if the limiting belief was "making money is hard", I would come up with "making money is fun and easy".

The new belief may feel or sound untrue for you at the moment, but that's because the "table" doesn't yet have "legs" under it to support it.

The next step is to come up with examples and reasons why this new empowering belief is now true. Each thing you come up with will act as a new leg for the table.

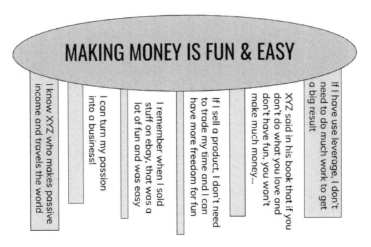

Come up with as many things as you can, but at least 10 minimum. By the end of this exercise, you'll feel a lot more certain about your new empowering belief.

At this stage, your new belief is still a fragile seedling and can easily become uprooted or damaged by your environment. To strengthen it, we need to move on to the final step...

STEP 4: Conditioning & Repetition

Through repetition, we condition ourselves with certain thoughts and behaviors that become habits.

We need to create a thought habit and reinforce this new empowering belief in our subconscious mind so it takes proper root there and will give us the results we want in our life.

226

You can also use affirmations to condition your mind. Affirmations are usually positive statements that are repeated with attention, focus and feeling over and over again until it becomes a subconscious thought pattern.

Affirmations are a powerful way to condition our mindset and strengthen a new belief.

Make sure your affirmations are phrased in the present tense and do not include negations. For example:

"I do not feel sad" is not a good affirmation, because the subconscious mind cannot think in negatives. It's like when I say to you "Do NOT think of an elephant". You just thought of an elephant!

Instead, a better affirmation is "I feel happy", because "happy" and "I" is what your mind will associate and what it will focus on.

The best time to do affirmations are first thing in the morning or right before sleep. This is when your subconscious is most receptive to suggestions.

The more often you can do your affirmations, the better. Start with 21 repetitions per affirmation, but make sure you are present, and put feeling and emotion into each repetition. That is the key.

You can choose 5 affirmations at a time, and do them for a few months until you feel they have integrated and become a part of you.

Subliminals & Supraliminals

Subliminal programming can also be a powerful way to condition your new beliefs in your subconscious.

Subliminal means below the threshold of sensation or consciousness. In the case of subliminal affirmations, your conscious mind is not aware of them, however, your subconscious mind hears them clearly.

You can use audio subliminals or audio supraliminals (where you have a track on top of the subliminal one that you can consciously hear).

Again, the best time to listen to these is first thing in the morning or right before sleep.

Tools & Resources:

I recommend checking out (vidtr.in/hypno) for subliminal & supraliminal tracks you can download and listen to.

You can also use a text-based subliminal software on your computer that constantly flashes text at millisecond intervals, too fast for your conscious mind to comprehend. A great program I use is "Free Subliminal Text"

Tools & Resources:

Free Subliminal Text - Free text subliminal software that runs in the background on your computer while you work. You can download here: vidtr.in/fst

---

Additional Ways to Eliminate Limiting Beliefs

One of my all-time favorite ways is a technique from the book SuperSleep™ by Teri D. Mahaney PhD. Also check out changeyourmind.com for more info.

Tools & Resources:

Change Your Mind - vidtr.in/cym

This website has all the scripts, CDs, and information you'll need to start benefitting from the SuperSleep™ technology.

This involves creating a script that you record with your own voice in a specific way, then adding relaxing music on top. You listen to this track while you sleep, during periods when your brainwaves are in the theta frequency (6–10 Hz), this is where the audio messages have the most effect on the subconscious mind.

During this time, you are literally reprogramming your mindset in a really powerful way and letting go of past limiting beliefs while conditioning the new empowering ones.

I've personally experienced major shifts and changes in my relationship with money, finances, and success after listening to these SuperSleep™ tracks I recorded. I've also had some pretty amazing experiences too that I know were as a result of listening to these tracks.

All I can say is if you're still skeptical, just try it for a month. Your resistance to trying something unknown is in itself a limiting belief. Take action regardless and let the results speak for themselves.

CHAPTER 24

The 30 Day Challenge

I f you want to build unstoppable momentum, overcome limiting be-liefs, improve your self confidence, immerse yourself in learning & mas-tering YouTube, as well as learn how to produce consistent video content, then this challenge is for you!

It's not for the faint of heart, so before you discard it, remember that **if you do what is easy, life becomes hard, but if you do what is hard, life becomes easy.** This is what my mentor taught me and it's so true.

In this chapter, I'll go through my experience of the 30-day challenge and what I did. Then I will give you some ideas and action steps to start with your own 30-day challenge.

My "Impossible" 30-Day Challenge

The 30-day challenge Mark tasked me with was to create 30 blogs, each targeting a specific niche that solves a big problem, and then write 5 articles for each blog targeting a long tail keyword phrase.

Each of the 5 articles would link to an affiliate product that was related to the niche. To get traffic, I was to create 12 YouTube videos for each blog, each targeting a long tail keyword phrase. My goal was to rank the videos to get the traffic.

In summary, I had to create 30 blogs, 150 articles, and 360 YouTube videos in 30 days and generate $1,000 as a result.

I was like "SERIOUSLY?!" He's like "Yeah, it's called a challenge for a reason!". OK, so even though I didn't have the £240 I needed to buy the 30 domains, and I had no idea how I was going to make it work, I said "YES" to the challenge and would figure out how to make it happen as I go.

After choosing the niches for the websites, with Mark's help, I set the start date for my 30-day challenge. It was September 2nd, 2016. That Saturday morning I was really excited to start creating the videos. I bought some animation software, VSL (video sales letter) software, and everything I *thought* I would need to make the "perfect" video.

One hour later, I finished creating my first video of the challenge. It was a 1-minute kinetic typography video and it totally sucked. I was like, how the hell am I going to create 12 videos a day if it takes 1 hour to create each one, ON TOP of my full time day job?!

The answer was simple. I had to become more **resourceful** and **creative**, and that was the only way I was going to make it work.

So I tried to become faster at creating the next few videos. Turns out, it still took way too long. I even went as far as creating a video sales letter script template, which I passed through a text-to-speech program, which then automatically created VSL videos.

They turned out hideous, sounded like a robot, and it <u>still</u> took a long time by the time everything was completed. This just wasn't going to work...

At that point I gave up. I emailed Mark a long email saying why it was "impossible" for me to do the challenges and then I curled up in my bed and felt depressed for the rest of the weekend.

I had lost hope. I told my friends and family about it and every one of them said, "That's crazy! Why are you so hard on yourself? That's a crazy challenge, don't do it." But something very interesting happened...

I realized that, even though these people may be very well-meaning, they don't know my dream, they don't understand this journey I'm on - I'm going to prove them wrong, I'm not going to give up, and I will find a way no matter what!

So Mark got another email from me that Sunday, saying that I have changed my mind and will do the challenge after all.

I got an email that Monday morning that really booted me into shape and basically said "man up, and just do it, make it happen". So I sucked it up and went back to it.

At this point I was a few days behind my targets so I had to catch up quite rapidly.

I needed to figure out how to create videos quickly... Then it struck me - why don't I just do "talking head" videos with me in front of the camera? It's not something I wanted to do, because I felt quite uncomfortable talking about many of the subjects, but I knew I needed to get out of my comfort zone and just do it.

I came up with a plan to do keyword research, shot 5 x one-minute call to action videos, and then 7 x value focused videos. I got the content ideas by literally plugging the keyword into Google and pulling up an authority blog post, for example "3 ways to lose weight naturally" and used those 3 things as talking points. It worked really well and I was able to soon shoot 12 videos in about 2 hours.

I created the blogs in batches, so whenever I got a bit more money from website clients I was doing on the side, I bought batches of domains, and then mass-installed the Wordpress blog software, themes, plugins and configured them.

For the 150 articles, I had to outsource them. I went on Upwork.com and posted a job saying I needed 150 articles of 500 words, all done in 30 days with strict time schedules and only a budget of $150 USD. I got one applicant who turned out to be one of my e-book writers I had hired 3 or 4 months previously.

She was committed and ended up completely the job on time.

Everyday I would choose 5 new keywords, come up with the article titles, and send it to her along with the affiliate link to add into the content.

Then I would publish the previous day's articles and find royalty free stock photos on Pixabay.com to enhance the look.

Every day, that's all I would do between my job, at every spare moment on the bus, train, lunch breaks and evenings - create videos, keyword research, publish the articles, and film and upload the videos. It was crazy.

30 days later, it was October 2nd and I managed to finish the last batch of videos, articles and blogs. I had completed everything within 30 days exactly. **I had turned something I had thought "impossible" into something possible.**

Although I had not generated any money during this time, I had learned so much from this experience and transformed my beliefs. I think it was Mark's aim for me to learn from the experience and "toughen up". I ended up developing a stronger work ethic, I became more resourceful, and I realized what did and didn't work on YouTube.

Your 30 Day Challenge

Now, it's your turn. Below are some 30-day challenges that you can choose and some advice for each to get you started.

It really comes down to being resourceful, creative, and becoming a better problem solver. You need to have an attitude of "I'll do whatever it takes".

A challenge is called a challenge for a reason, because you literally need to start thinking differently to overcome the blocks that are stopping you from achieving the goal.

Here are 5 different 30-day challenges you can choose from:

1) Get 1,000 YouTube subscribers in 30 days
2) Make $1,000 thanks to YouTube in 30 days
3) Rank 100 videos on the first page of YouTube in 30 days
4) Build an email list of 500 email subscribers thanks to YouTube in 30 days
5) Create & publish 360 videos on YouTube in 30 days

Get 1,000 YouTube subscribers in 30 days

In this challenge, your focus will be on getting subscribers. This will require you to get a lot of views on your videos by ranking them on first page of YouTube, sharing your videos on social media platforms, and even embedding them on other websites with lots of targeted traffic.

Each video needs to deliver a lot of value, be super engaging, and have a clear call to action to invite the viewer to subscribe.

You may even decide that collaborating with other YouTubers in your niche may bring faster results by leveraging their subscriber base.

Make $1,000 thanks to YouTube in 30 days

Your goal is to generate $1,000 in 30 days from YouTube traffic. Making money from YouTube ads are out of the question for a brand new channel, so the best strategies here are offering or reviewing affiliate products, or building an email list by giving away something for free, and then offering a product or service.

If you think in terms of numbers, it would be far easier to make 5 sales at $200 each than 200 sales of $5 each. The latter would require much more traffic and views.

The best way to get lots of clicks is to rank videos for keywords with a lot of searches so you can get your views up. Then, have a clear call to action near the end of the video to invite the viewers to click on the link in the description.

Rank 100 videos on the first page of YouTube in 30 days

This challenge revolves specifically around ranking videos on the first page of YouTube. Keep in mind, to get 100 videos on the first page, you may have to optimize 200 or more videos, as not all will successfully reach the top 20 for the keyword.

Apply the strategies outlined in part 2 of this book to optimize your videos for most views. The more effort you put into optimizing each video, the higher the chances it has in ranking on the first page.

Make sure you also choose keywords that have a good balance between competition and search volume.

Build an email list of 500 email subscribers thanks to YouTube in 30 days

Your goal is to build an email list of 500 subscribers thanks to YouTube traffic. This can be accomplished by getting your viewers to click on a link in the description, which leads them to a landing page offering a free gift (pdf/ebook/video) in exchange for their email. I suggest using ClickFunnels or LeadPages to create landing pages.

Again, to get the clicks, you'll need a lot of views, which means ranking your videos on the first page of YouTube or Google.

If you estimate a 20% conversion rate of subscribers to clicks, you would need to generate 2,500 clicks from your videos. Let's say you have a 10% click through rate on your videos. That means, you'll need to get 25,000 views on your views in 30 days to reach this number.

Before you get shocked, you can easily break this down into something that sounds more realistic. To get 25,000 views, all you need is 120 videos at 209 views each, or 240 videos at 105 views each.

If you create 4-8 videos a day and rank them on the first page of YouTube for decent keywords, you can definitely reach this goal.

Create & publish 360 videos on YouTube in 30 days

This challenge focuses purely on content creation and consistency. It will challenge your creativity, endurance, and self-discipline.

If you break it down, it is only 12 videos a day. They don't have to be long or perfect. 1-3 minutes, sharing a valuable tip or useful information, with you in front of the camera will suffice.

Ideally target a keyword for each video, so you get into the habit of optimizing your videos as well.

CHAPTER 25

Your Next Steps

N ow that you've finished reading this book, it is just the beginning of your YouTube journey. In order for this information to create real lasting results in your life and your business, **you must take action - <u>consistently</u>!**

A lot of people know what to do, but make excuses as to why they can't do it. Very few people do what they know, no matter what life throws at them. I hope you're the latter kind of person.

For more content, make sure you watch all the exclusive YouTube VIP interviews, explore the links, use the tools, connect with and follow the experts, and check out the main website http://videotrafficinsider.com for more resources and content.

If you're looking for more in-depth training, then check out the last few pages where you can **join a free webinar** or check out the **How To Make $100,000 Per Year Thanks To YouTube Home Study Course**, which will go into even more detail and multiply & accelerate your results.

CHAPTER 26

Glossary

A/B split tests - Also known as just "split tests", these are tests where traffic is split equally between two slightly different pages A and B, to see which page gets a higher conversion rate for the purpose of making incremental improvements.

AdSense - This is the name of the ad program that pays YouTubers for displaying ads on their videos.

Affiliate dashboard - This is the part of an affiliate account where you can view your commissions, traffic data and other statistics.

Affiliate link - This is a unique link that is assigned to your affiliate account when you sign up which tracks the number of sales you have made through your this link.

Autosuggestions - These are recommended popular searches that automatically drop down in the search bar.

Backlinks - Any link from an external web page pointing back to the page you are optimizing.

Blackhat - The usage of optimization strategies, techniques and tactics which are against the terms of service of the platforms they are being used on for the purpose of gaining a competitive advantage over other listings.

Boosting - The process of driving an initial burst of traffic and/or social engagement to a video to help it rank much faster.

Buyer demand - A need that your target audience has that they are willing to pay money to find a solution for.

Call to action - A clear command to the viewer or reader that tells them exactly what action to take, usually located near the end of the video or at the end of a page.

Click Through Rate (CTR) - The number of clicks a link gets divided by the number of impressions or views it gets.

Closed captions - this is text that appears over the video to mirror the voice and can be turned on or off.

CPC - Cost per click is the metric that shows what the average amount a pay per click (PPC) advertiser will pay for a click on their advert.

Customer avatar - This is a detailed description of your ideal customer, which includes their major pain points, demographics, desires, and personality.

Embeds/Embedding/Embedded videos - These are videos that are inserted into web pages outside of the primary video platform.

Evergreen - Anything that stays fresh, popular, or relevant regardless of the passing of time.

Exact URL - The full URL, and not just the root domain.

Greyhat - Any tactic that is not Blackhat or Whitehat, but in-between.

High retention views - Videos that have been watched at least 70% or more of the way through their entire duration.

Keyword positions - The location of a video or website in the search list results for a particular keyword.

Keyword - A query that is made up of one or more words which is typed into the search bar.

Landing page - A page on a website which the visitor first lands on and is designed to direct the visitor to the next action, which may be to subscribe to a newsletter, download something, or purchase a product, for example.

Leads - Contact information (usually email address) of a prospect that has shown interest in your information, product or service.

Leverage - The process of getting a bigger output using a smaller input. For example, automating the sales process allows you to make more sales without taking any more of your time, is considered high leverage.

Marketing funnel - A consumer focused marketing model, which shows the possible customer journey towards the purchase of a product or service. Usually a marketing funnel has a lower priced offer leading to a mid-priced offer and finally to a high priced offer.

Meta or Meta Data - The details of a video, which includes the title, description and tags.

Natural/Organic - A term used in search, meaning non-paid-for traffic in the search engines.

Niche - Products, services, or interests that appeal to a small, specialized section of a market.

Off-page SEO - Any factors that help to increase the search engine performance that are not related to elements on the website.

On-page SEO - Any factors that help to increase the search engine performance that are related to elements on the website.

Optin pages - Also known as lead capture pages, these pages are designed for the purpose of capturing a prospect's contact details in exchange for something else of value, like a free download.

Positioning - To portray or regard someone as a particular type of person.

PPC - Pay per click advertising where advertisers pay for clicks to their adverts.

Rank tracking software - Software that tracks the positions of websites or videos in the search results for given keywords.

Ranking factors - Factors, which directly or indirectly affect the positions of the video (or website) in the search results.

Ranking videos - The process of optimizing your videos for the goal of reaching the highest position (closest to first result) in the search results.

Relevancy - How closely related a search result or video is to a given keyword.

Screencast - A digital recording of computer screen output, also known as a video screen capture, often containing audio narration.

SEO - Search engine optimization is the process of optimizing a website or video to appear as close to the first position of search results for a given keyword.

Social signals - Likes, shares, votes, pins, or views on Facebook, Twitter, LinkedIn or other social media sites that filter out to the various search engines and affect the SEO rankings.

Target market - A particular group of consumers at which a product or service is aimed.

URL - Uniform Resource Locator is the address of a World Wide Web page.

Video rank - The search result position of a video in YouTube, Google or other search engine that supports videos.

Vlogging - A blog in which the postings are primarily in video form.

Whitehat - The usage of optimization strategies, techniques and tactics that focus on a human audience opposed to search engines and follows search engine rules and policies.

Free Webinar

Join me **LIVE** on a **FREE** webinar where you can interact with me, ask me questions, and learn about the latest YouTube & video marketing strategies and tactics to get you more free targeted traffic and make you more money.

I host these webinars regularly, so make sure to choose a suitable date and time and sign up via the following link:

http://vidtr.in/webinar

Specific video traffic topics may vary slightly over time, but this will be the page I keep updated regularly, so you can check it out.

Home Study Course

If you enjoyed this book but want to dive deeper into the tactics and strategies I, and other YouTube & video marketing experts around the world use every day to get maximum results, then I've got the perfect next step for you...

I have created the **How To Make $100,000 Per Year Thanks To YouTube Home Study Course** for readers who want to "look over my shoulder" and follow along in more detail about how to master YouTube & video marketing.

The course includes over 46+ step-by-step videos spanning 9 hours of value-packed content and lots of additional resources, tools, templates, and training materials that will make sure you absorb the maximum amount of knowledge you need to get the results you desire.

You'll also be able to join a community of other YouTubers and video marketers who you can connect with and learn from.

I will also reveal a few of my top insider-only secrets in the course that will further boost and accelerate your results on YouTube.

You can check out and learn more about the course here:

http://vidtr.in/webinar

ABOUT THE AUTHOR

Gabriel Both is from Nova Scotia, Canada and did his Bachelors of Computer Science degree at Acadia University.

He has practiced Internet Marketing since 2012 and has worked with international clients all over the world including well-known brands such as Volvo, Harrods, Waterstones, Virgin Active, Spar, and many others.

His main areas of expertise are SEO and video marketing on YouTube. You can connect with Gabriel on Facebook here: http://facebook.com/gabe.both

Made in the USA
Lexington, KY
26 April 2019